THE POPE, HIS BANKER,
AND VENICE

THE POPE,
HIS BANKER,
AND VENICE

FELIX GILBERT

HARVARD UNIVERSITY PRESS
CAMBRIDGE, MASSACHUSETTS
LONDON, ENGLAND
1980

Library of Congress Cataloging in Publication Data

Gilbert, Felix, 1905-
    The Pope, his banker, and Venice.

    Includes bibliographical references and index.
        1. Venice—History—1508-1797. 2. Cambrai,
League of, 1508. 3. Venice—Foreign relations—
Catholic Church. 4. Catholic Church—Relations—
(diplomatic) with Venice. 5. Julius II, Pope,
1443-1513. 6. Chigi, Agostino. 1466-1520.
7. Papacy—History—1447-1565. I. Title.
DG678.25.G54   945′.31   80-13062
ISBN 0-674-68975-5

Acknowledgments

The research that resulted in the composition of this book began when, in the course of a study on the impact of the War of
the League of Cambrai on the political and social life of Venice, I
came upon a series of documents on loan negotiations between
the Venetian government and the wealthy banker Agostino
Chigi. These documents had much to say about the diplomacy
and financial policy of the Renaissance. I came to realize that the
story connected with these documents could be fully elucidated
only by research extending beyond Venice into the archives and
libraries of Rome and other Italian cities. As it turned out, the
story led far beyond the scope of my original project, and required separate treatment.

As in earlier work on Italian Renaissance history, I owe a
great debt of gratitude to Italian archivists and librarians. I
would like to express my thanks to the directors, archivists, and
librarians of the Archivio di Stato, the Biblioteca Marciana, and
the Biblioteca Correr in Venice; and in particular I would like to
mention the advice I received from the Direttrice of the Archivio
di Stato, Dr. Maria Francesca Tiepolo. In Rome I worked in the
Archivio di Stato, in the Biblioteca Vaticana, and in the Archivio
Secreto Vaticano; my special thanks are due to the Viceprefetto
of the Biblioteca Vaticana, Monsignor Ruysschaert. I also
worked, although only briefly, in the Archivi di Stato of Florence and Siena; my work in Siena was facilitated by information
I received from Professor Giuliano Catino of the University of
Siena. As on previous occasions, Dr. Gino Corti helped me with
his great knowledge of Italian archives, and I used copies he had

v

made of some manuscripts. An interesting document from the Vatican archives was placed at my disposal by Peter Partner of Winchester College, and this document led me to files that proved to be of great usefulness. Professor John H. Hale permitted me to read the manuscript of his work on the Venetian military organization so that I was able to check and to correct my statements about military affairs.

When I was Kennedy Guest Professor at Smith College in 1975-76, I presented parts of the book in public lectures which were followed by helpful discussions.

Mary R. Gilbert gave much time to a thorough examination and critical review of each chapter as soon as it was finished; there is no page that has not been improved in consequence of her work. John H. Elliott of the Institute for Advanced Study and Arno Mayer of Princeton University read the entire manuscript and made many valuable suggestions. I enjoyed working with the Harvard University Press, and especially having the advice and support of Dr. Aida Donald.

Contents

THE PAPAL STATES AND THE REPUBLIC OF VENICE, EARLY SIXTEENTH CENTURY

Fiefs of the Pope

MILAN

Bergamo
Brescia
Milan •
Agnadello Lago di Garda
Crema
Cremona
Po River

FRIULI

Vicenza Treviso
Verona Mestre
Montagnana Padua
Este Venice
Adige R.
Po R.
Mirandola
Ferrara
Comacchio

ISTRIA

Adriatic Sea

Genoa
GENOA

ROMAGNA
Bologna Ravenna
Faenza Cervia

Rimini
Pesaro
Fano
Senigallia
Urbino Ancona
THE MARCHES

Pisa
Florence
FLORENCE
Siena •

Ligurian Sea

Perugia Assisi
UMBRIA
Orvieto
Spoleto

SIENA

ELBA

CORSICA

Viterbo
PATRIMONY
OF ST. PETER
Porto Ercole
Tolfa
Civitavecchia
Tiber R.
Ostia Rome
CAMPAGNA AND
MARITTIMA

KINGDOM
OF
NAPLES

north

SAVOY
GENOA
CORSICA
Genoa
VENETIAN REPUBLIC
KINGDOM OF HUNGARY
Ragusa
PAPAL STATES
KINGDOM OF NAPLES
KINGDOM OF SARDINIA
KINGDOM OF SICILY

0   50   100   150 km
0   50   100   150 miles

THE POPE, HIS BANKER,
AND VENICE

--◦◦{ I }◦◦--

Venice in the War
of the League of Cambrai

THE HALL of the Doge's palace, where the Venetian Senate
assembled, is adorned by a large painting of Palma Giovane's celebrating the victory of Venice over the League of Cambrai. Sansovino's *Venetia città nobilissima*, the celebrated sixteenth-century guidebook to the historic monuments and art
treasures of Venice, gives the following description of this painting: "In the center stands the Doge Leonardo Loredan and next
to him Venezia and her lion. Venezia draws a rapier against another young woman, clad in a coat of mail, a helmet on her
head, riding a bull; she represents Europe and holds a shield on
which are depicted the coats-of-arms of the princes allied against
Venice. In the corner of the painting, two other figures can be
seen: Peace and Plenty, which will flourish under the Doge's
wise reign. Hovering above are two personifications of Victory,
holding wreaths of olives in their hands. Padua is outlined on the
horizon because it was the first city that Venice reconquered on
the terra firma."[1]

The War of the League of Cambrai—named after the town in
the Netherlands where in 1508 the alliance against Venice was
concluded—lasted from 1509 to 1517.[2] The painting is sugges-
tive of a situation that existed for only four or five months in the
year 1509: Venice was standing alone against the most powerful
states of Europe—France, Germany, England, Spain, and the
Pope, who used not only his armies but also his spiritual weapon
of excommunication. In these early months of the war, the possession of Padua was crucial. After the disastrous defeat of the
Venetian army at Agnadello on May 14, 1509, Venice lost all its

1

widespread possessions on the terra firma, and the nadir of Venetian power was reached when even Padua—whose conquest in 1405 had signified the beginning of Venetian expansion over the terra firma—fell to the enemy early in June 1509. Thus the reconquest of Padua by a surprise attack on July 17, six weeks after it had been lost, was considered a turning point, signifying that Venice would rise again. In the following months Padua withstood a siege by Maximilian, the German king, and most of the terra firma was back in Venetian hands when military operations ceased with the approach of winter. Venice had survived. Yet the war dragged on, and Venice continued to pass through periods of great danger. The campaign in the summer of 1510 was almost a repetition of what had happened in 1509: the terra firma again was lost although, this time, Padua was held. In one essential fact, however, the situation was different from that of the preceding year: Venice was no longer isolated.

Immediately after the defeat at Agnadello, the Venetians had made a strong effort to break up the alliance that had been formed against them, and this effort was bearing fruit. It seemed to the Venetians that their best hope lay in trying to bring about a change in the attitude of Pope Julius II. To show their goodwill, they handed over to papal representatives the towns in the Romagna which they had occupied after the downfall of Cesare Borgia's rule in 1503—that move had angered the Pope because he claimed these areas as part of the papal states. The surrender of these territories to papal authority was followed by the appointment of ambassadors who went to Rome to beg the Pope to lift the excommunication of Venice and to sue for peace. At first, the Pope was unyielding, but he could not fail to see that the continued existence of Venice as a power was an absolute necessity in order to prevent France from gaining complete control over northern Italy. Furthermore the Pope saw in the reconquest of Padua and in the successful defense of the city against Maximilian's attack an indication that Venice still had resources that might be of great value in a struggle against France. So, in February 1510, after long and difficult negotiations in which Venice was forced to accept stringent conditions, the excommunication was lifted and peace was reestablished between the Pope and Venice.

Thus, in the midsummer of 1510, when the Venetians again were hard pressed and had lost much of the terra firma, the Pope intervened. Swiss Landsknechte, hired by the Pope, moved against the French from the north, and papal troops moved against Ferrara, the French king's most loyal ally and Venice's neighbor and old enemy. These maneuvers were of limited success. Venice gained breathing space, but Verona and a good part of the terra firma remained in French hands. The intervention of the Landsknechte brought no relief; after a brief advance, they withdrew. Ferrara proved to be too strongly defended. Nevertheless, military cooperation between Venice and the Pope had now been established and grew stronger in the following months. The Pope, impatient with the lack of progress during the summer campaign, insisted on prosecuting the war against Ferrara during the winter, and he himself went to Bologna and then, to give the campaign impetus, on to the troops operating against Ferrara. Again Ferrara proved to be beyond reach, but the papal army surrounded Mirandola, a mountain fortress protecting the road to the French headquarters in Milan. In this operation, the papal troops were supported by one part of the Venetian army; the other half of the army was stationed further north guarding against advances of French troops from the west and of German troops from the north. This was the precarious situation in February 1511 when our story begins. The French had been rather passive during the winter, but it could be expected that, with the coming of spring, the customary time for the beginning of a new campaign, they would take the initiative in a new offensive.

P AINTINGS in public buildings commemorate the great moments and the heroic deeds of the past; they are intended to encourage the viewer to reflect on events that demonstrate the value of strength and courage. But wars are more than a series of armed clashes. Military operations are only one part of a complex web of diplomatic negotiations, administrative regulations, and economic measures. During the Italian Renaissance, the diplomatic and political aspects of war were frequently more decisive than military operations, and the War of the League of Cambrai is a typical example of this, its outcome being finally decided by changes in alliances and power groups, by the capacity of rulers to mobilize their resources rather than by campaigns and battles. Palma's painting in the ducal palace commemorating Venice's victory in the war hangs over the door leading from the hall in which the Senate met to the room of the Collegio. Although it is unlikely that this spot was consciously chosen, it is strangely meaningful: the direction of affairs during the war fell to the two assemblies whose meeting halls were connected by that door.[3]

The Collegio was the most authoritative body in the Venetian structure of councils and magistracies; when we talk about actions of the "Venetian government," we are referring to decisions of the Collegio. The Collegio had increased in size over the centuries, and by the early sixteenth century it had twenty-six members. The most ancient component of the Collegio consisted of the Doge and his counselors—one from each of the six districts (*sestiere*) into which Venice was divided. Later the Collegio was enlarged by the addition of the three heads of the Quarantia, which was the forty-man appeals court in criminal and civil cases. A further addition was the sixteen "Wise Men," members of the Council of Savi, who, by the time of the War of the League of Cambrai, were probably the most important element in the Collegio. They had different administrative functions and, accordingly, were unequal in their influence. Five of the Savi, usually young nobles, still inexperienced in government affairs, were in charge of navy supplies and supervised trade and overseas colonies; they were called Savi ai Ordini. Five other members of the Council of Savi, called Savi di Terra Firma, administered the Venetian possessions in northern Italy, organized the army, and directed the financial agencies. The most powerful members of the Council of Savi were, as their name indicates, the six Savi Grandi. They had the overall control over the execution of policy decisions.

Usually in the mornings, the full Collegio assembled, discussed whatever new information had come in, and decided on the measures to be taken. Then the Savi were commissioned to issue the required orders and to draft the necessary replies and instructions. If foreign affairs demanded action that had to be handled with particular discretion or urgency, they were sometimes entrusted to the heads of the Council of Ten (the Dieci), originally a magistry in charge of internal security, but which in the sixteenth century began to extend its functions into the areas of foreign policy and finance.

In the next stage of the policy-making process, the Pregadi— or the Senate, as this assembly was officially styled—were consulted and could make their weight felt. The measures the Savi prepared, including all the instructions to Venetian ambassadors abroad, had to be submitted for approval to the Pregadi. When they were considered to be particularly important and it was feared that they might encounter strong opposition in the Pregadi, they were presented in the name of the entire Collegio. Usually, however, they were proposed in the name of the Council of Savi or of that group of the Savi in whose fields of competence the suggested measure fell. This did not mean that these proposals had not been approved by the entire Collegio and did not have its authority behind them.

The manner by which a political decision was reached has two notable features: proposals were never made by an individual, but in the name of an agency or council, and it was understood that behind them stood the authority of the entire government.

It was considered important to give the appearance of unity and a common will.

This impression is deceptive; in reality, differences of opinion and sharp tensions existed among the Venetian political leaders. They are not easy to discover or define because of a tendency toward concealment. Nevertheless, there are various indications of their existence in the sources. A Savio might propose an amendment to an instruction which suggests that he is in favor of a different approach. In the documents presented to the Pregadi, all proposals carried in the left margin the names of their sponsors; sometimes a Savio placed after his name a short remark that he does not agree with this particular proposal; sometimes an important member of the Collegio, whose concern with the subject matter under discussion is known, is noted as absent. In pursuing such instances of counterproposals, disapprovals, or absences over a stretch of time, a picture of conflicts and of groupings emerges. Sometimes such hints can be substantiated through statements in the two great diaries that cover the period of the War of the League of Cambrai—those of Marino Sanudo[4] and Girolamo Priuli.[5] Insofar as attempts to penetrate the harmonious surface of Venetian politics are concerned, these diarists complement each other. Priuli is quite frank in outlining differing and opposing views, but is too discreet to affix names to them; Sanudo enjoyed reporting the clashes among leading personalities, but is rather vague in describing the arguments. Only at critical moments can we recognize how differences over issues are entangled with clashes between personalities. Much about the conflicts and tensions in Venetian politics and their connection with personal rivalries remains in the dark.

The extent of the power over Venetian politics which the Collegio and Pregadi possessed during the War of the League of Cambrai becomes more clear when the functions and activities of these two bodies are compared with those of the most famous and usually highest-ranked institution of the Venetian government: the Great Council (Maggior Consiglio). Certainly, sovereignty rested with the Great Council; every Venetian noble above the age of twenty-five belonged to it, and at the time of the War of the League of Cambrai it had more than 2500 members, something like 10 percent of the male population of the city in the same age group.[6] Since its "closing"[7] early in the fourteenth century, the membership of the Great Council had more than doubled, and the increase in size reduced its effectiveness and influence. It was clumsy to manage, and impossible to handle in weekly meetings the incessant stream of business with thoroughness, dispatch, and secrecy. It remained a firm rule that approval by the Great Council was needed for any changes that concerned the Venetian constitutional structure and the relations among the various government agencies and councils; this competence ensured the Great Council's embodiment of Venetian sovereignty and guardian of the Venetian political tradition. Its active participation in the conduct of politics centered on its right to elect important officials: the main officials of the city of Venice, the various governors and administrators in the towns of the terra firma and of Venice's overseas possessions, the members of the Pregadi, the Quarantia, the Council of Ten, and the Doge.

This description might convey the impression of the Great Council's firm grip over the entire governmental apparatus. But this would be misleading. Only a limited number of nobles had the qualifications fitting them to hold the office of counselor or member of the Ten. Also, the dependence of the Pregadi on the Great Council was more apparent than real. The Pregadi consisted of 150 to 200 men;[8] a good number of them were high officials who, because of the office they held, were entitled to attend the meetings of the Pregadi but without the right to vote. The bulk of the Pregadi were the 120 members whom the Great Council elected annually during the months of August and September. Still, the Great Council had free choice only in a nominal way; it had become customary to reelect those who had been in the Pregadi in the preceding year. Some changes took place: those members who died had to be replaced, and vacancies were

7

created when members of the Pregadi received appointments or were chosen for missions that took them away from Venice. Sometimes the Great Council did assert its right of free choice. When there was a military defeat or when Venice was forced to conclude a humiliating agreement, those who were considered to have been the chief advocates of the policy that led to failure were not reelected. But this was rare, and exclusion from the Pregadi was usually only temporary. Members of the Pregadi could feel they belonged to a body that was not responsible to any other council, and that they were entitled to determine and conduct whatever policies they wanted.

During the War of the League of Cambrai, the political role of the Great Council diminished. With the loss of the terra firma, the number of government positions filled by election to the Great Council was sharply reduced. The financial advantages of holding positions on the terra firma made their possession very attractive—not so much for the rich leading citizens as for the greater numbers of "poor nobles." When enemy occupation removed the need for election by the Great Council to these positions, many nobles lost interest in its proceedings and, during the war, meetings were poorly attended. Moreover, wartime exigencies unavoidably shifted the weight of leadership to the Senate. The war required daily attendance to business and quick decisions, and although the distribution of the great majority of government offices was in the hands of the Great Council, those that were of particular importance for the conduct of war were not. First of all the Council of Savi was regarded as a committee of the Senate, and so its members were elected by the Pregadi. The Pregadi also elected the diplomatic representatives of the Venetian government; their activities were crucial for the conduct of the war. But the Pregadi also elected the men who had chief responsibility for the military operations: the provveditori. For the duration of their appointment they stayed with the troops, in close contact with the condottiere. It was their responsibility to act as intermediaries between the Collegio and the condottiere, to transmit to the condottiere the instructions of the Venetian government and to report to the government about the military situation and operational plans. To be a provveditore in a successful campaign could be the steppingstone to the highest office; for instance, Gritti, one of the most efficient provveditori in the War of the League of Cambrai, later was elected Doge. It was also a risky position because the provveditore was frequently held responsible for failure or defeat. Finally, the Pregadi had a decisive say in what, at the time, was characterized as "the sinews of war": finances—they had to pass on proposals to levy new taxes.

The most important decisions in wartime were made in the Collegio and, particularly, in the Council of Savi; the Pregadi gave the final stamp. However, fundamental reexamination and reconsideration of an issue almost never took place in the deliberations of the Pregadi. The members of the Collegio, particularly the Savi Grandi, led the discussion in the Pregadi. They had the right to speak first, and as a matter of fact it was rare for senators who did not belong to the Collegio or to the Council of Ten or who did not hold a high official position even to address the Senate.

Nevertheless, the Collegio and the Savi were not executive agencies in contrast to a "deliberative" or "legislative" Senate. In all these bodies—actually even in the Great Council—the executive, deliberative, and legislative functions, which we are now accustomed to separate, were combined.

This system might seem to have invited temptation for a few, by dominating the Savi and Pregadi, to take control of the government and exclude the rest of the nobility from power. But institutional arrangements existed which were intended to prevent the consolidation of power in the hands of a small group. The most important precaution was the rotation of offices: the term of office was strictly limited. Average tenure of office was six months. A man whose term had ended could not be elected to the same office again until as many months had passed as he had held office. Consequently, the membership of the Council of Savi changed frequently, although the dates at which the various members entered the Council were staggered so that continuity of policy could be preserved. Limitation of tenure and rotation of offices were customary in the city republics of Renaissance Italy, and the legislation on this matter in Florence was not very different from that in Venice. But some regulations intended to hinder the formation of groups or parties were uniquely Venetian. Most important was the legislation against what was called *broglio*, a private agreement among members of the Great Council about whom to vote for. The fact that the members of the Pregadi were usually reelected from year to year, so that this group was comprised of men who had joined the Senate at different times and under different circumstances, also helped to impede the prevalence of one particular group or party.

The condemnation of factious struggles, the need for acting in cooperation and harmony, was imposed not only by institutional arrangements or by laws and penalties. The attitude had roots in the Venetian past. Venice's nobility was a coherent entity, a class set apart and above the great mass of other people living in the city. The power and wealth of its families were based on naval exploits that had been common undertakings, and government organization and regulation were still essential to the trading enterprises by which Venice lived. The feeling of being a distinct and united group, bound together by a common fate, was personified in the nine officials who, in dignity, surpassed the members of all other magistracies and councils: the Procuratores di San Marco.[9]

Apart from the Doge, these men were the only officials who, once elected, held office for life; from the fourteenth century on, no Venetian noble ever became Doge who had not been a Procurator of San Marco. The original and ancient function of this office was to take care of the church of Venice's patron saint and of the land that surrounded the church and belonged to it. But soon the Procurators were also entrusted with the property and money that came to the Church of San Marco through legacies; they were charged with administering the goods of orphans and minors. The possessions and the amounts of money they came to control were considerable and made them a financial power in Venice. As the work involved in the fulfillment of their functions increased, so did their numbers; by the fifteenth century there were nine, and a division of labor took place: three Procurators, called "Procuratores de supra," were concerned with all issues connected with the building of San Marco; another group of three Procurators administered the estates left to San Marco by people who had lived on the church side of the Grand Canal—these were the Procurators "de citra"; and the estates from the other side of the Canal were managed by the three Procurators "de ultra." Originally there was fear that the wealth the Procurators controlled would give them so much power that they would exert a dominating influence on Venetian politics, and accordingly Procurators were not allowed to hold political office. But as the Venetian governmental apparatus became larger and more complex, and other magistrates began to control extended areas of public administration, the exclusion of the Procurators—men of great experience and authority—from officeholding no longer seemed justifiable. From the fifteenth century on, the Procurators of San Marco were automatically members of the Senate; they were employed as ambassadors, as provveditori, and as commanders of the fleet. Finally, they could also be elected to the Council of Savi, although the number of Procurators in this council was limited to two, who were to come from different groups; there could not be two from "de supra" or "de citra" or "de ultra" simultaneously in the Savi.

The Venetian government is frequently described as a pyramid. The base is formed by the Great Council; on this base stands the Senate; the structure gradually thins out to the peak, consisting of the Doge and his counselors. Its simplicity makes this analogy very attractive, and it has been widely used because it also has a long and respected history. In his famous description

11

of the Venetian Republic written in the decade after the War of the League of Cambrai, Gasparo Contarini emphasized the organic coherence of the Venetian constitution: it contained all three classical forms of government—democracy, aristocracy, and monarchy—and therefore was a realization of what ancient writers had judged to be the ideal constitution.[10]

But the image of the pyramid is misleading. Certainly, connections and interdependencies existed among the councils and agencies of the Venetian governmental apparatus, but they are somewhat tenuous—there is a strong tendency of each of the two large councils, and also of the other policymaking agencies, to form a gravitational center of their own, to cut out for themselves an area in which they had a free hand. Within the set frame, the various power centers rubbed against one another, each trying to enlarge its sphere of competence, and in this system of struggling forces, the balance frequently shifted. There is one general underlying trend in these institutional frictions: a constant movement toward a narrowing of the decisionmaking circle. The Great Council, originally the source of all power, had to concede part of its functions to the Senate; then the Collegio and the Savi began to take over many of the activities of the Senate; and, in the seventeenth and eighteenth centuries, the Council of Ten became all-powerful. The years of the War of the League of Cambrai turned out to be a crucial step in this development.

In the rivalries among the political leaders of Venice, differences on issues of policy were frequently entangled with struggles over procedure and legal competence. The value placed on observance of institutional arrangements touched on the very core of Venetian political life and had its origin in fundamental principles of Venetian political life. The nobles towered above all other groups of the population because they alone had the right to hold office. Gasparo Contarini stated with pride that, in Venice, no sumptuous tombs and no equestrian statues were erected to honor Venice's great leaders. To Contarini, this lack

12

of glorification of the individual was a sign of the nobility's modesty and selflessness. But he does not mention that praise of the exceptional faculties and achievements of an individual could also threaten the basic assumption of Venetian political life: the right of a hereditary class to a monopoly of power. It might be asked whether individuals of similar virtues were not also entitled to rule. The danger inherent in the eminence of one person had to be overcome by presenting the individual as a member of the system, by stressing his position as an officeholder. The visibility the Venetians gave to this relationship is proof of the importance they placed on fitting the individual into the institutional framework.[11]

The Procurators of San Marco were clearly recognizable by the velvet stoles they wore over their red robes. The robes of the senators were also red, but of a different hue. The Savi wore blue robes, and those of the members of the Council of Ten had particularly long sleeves. Nobles who held none of the higher government offices had to be content with black robes. This colorfulness in dress—which accords so well to the ever-changing light of Venice's sky and water—was frequently taken by outsiders as a further sign of the "miraculous" character of the Venetian political order. The willing acceptance of hierarchical distinctions in such visible form corresponded to the spirit of harmonious unity with which Venetian society was believed to be permeated.

But the emphasis on differences in dress can also be seen in another way: as a reflection of the continued existence of frictions and rivalries among the ruling elite, with each member insisting that he has his own rights and tasks, his own distinctive place. Such a perspective might not please those who see in Venetian history a glorious epic, as depicted in the halls of the ducal palace. But this more skeptical view seems nearer to reality when one takes a close look at individual episodes of Venetian history. At least that is what the events of the year 1511 seem to demonstrate.

--◦⊰ II ⊱◦--

Chigi in Venice:
The Crisis of the Spring of 1511

IN A DIARY ENTRY of February 3, 1511, Marino Sanudo
mentions that Agostino Chigi, an immensely wealthy Roman,
is on a visit to Venice.[1] Clearly, the fame of Chigi's wealth impressed Sanudo greatly, and in the following months he set
down in his diary whatever he heard about Chigi and his doings
in Venice. Later in February Sanudo has further information:
Chigi is a banker with capital of 100,000 ducats, and he holds
offices at the Curia which provide him with additional income.
He is staying in Venice at the Palazzo Nani in an apartment that
has been rented by a foreign merchant residing in Venice, Raphael Besalù, who was Chigi's agent in Venice. Sanudo has heard
that the purpose of Chigi's Venetian voyage is to get hold of a
Sienese banker, Alessandro di Franza, who owed Chigi 17,000
ducats. Chigi carried a brief from the Pope asking the Venetian
government to give Chigi all possible support and indeed the
Doge and his advisers promised to do whatever they could to aid
him. The government took energetic action; in order to obtain
Alessandro di Franza's account books, Franza's wife, a niece of
Pandolfo Petrucci, the ruler of Siena, was placed in custody.

It is clear that the Franza affair was of deep concern to Agostino Chigi. The man Sanudo calls Alessandro di Franza belonged
to the Spannocchi family, and the Spannocchi, originally from
Siena, as was Chigi, had been the great bankers at the Curia
under Popes Innocent VIII and Alexander VI.[2] At the beginning
of his career Chigi had been associated with them, but later conflicts and litigation had developed.

Nevertheless, it might be asked whether the possibility of col-

15

lecting a disputed debt, high indeed but hardly of crucial size for Chigi, was sufficient reason for a man of his importance to spend months in Venice. Chigi was continuously involved in the affairs of the Curia; he was a confidant of Pope Julius II, who had shown his gratitude by making the Chigis members of his own family, the della Rovere. And just at the time of his visit to Venice, Chigi, an active patron of the arts, was engaged in arranging for the construction of a most impressive memorial to his artistic interests: the Villa Farnesina.

Doubts that the suit against Alessandro di Franza was the only or the chief reason for Chigi's presence in Venice are reinforced by what Sanudo's entries indicate about the importance that Venetian patricians attached to Chigi's visit. On Sunday, February 23, 1511, Antonio Grimani, an influential figure in Venetian life and politics, gave a banquet in Chigi's honor. Grimani had had a most colorful career. After acquiring great wealth in business, he quickly advanced in the Venetian government service to become a Procurator of San Marco in 1494. But a few years later, when he was commander of the Venetian navy, the fleet was defeated by the Turks. Grimani was brought back to Venice in chains, and after a bitter trial he went in exile to Rome, where one of his sons was a Cardinal. After the Venetian defeat at Agnadello, he used the influence he had at the papal court in Venice's favor, and in July 1509 he was recalled from exile and was soon reestablished as Procurator of San Marco—the only man who was twice elected Procurator of San Marco. From 1509 to 1511 he served uninterruptedly as member of the Council of Savi and exerted great influence on Venetian policy. The Grimani—Antonio Grimani and two of his sons living in Rome, Cardinal Domenico Grimani and another cleric, Pietro Grimani, member of the Knights of Jerusalem—had been in close contact with Chigi in Rome, and it was natural therefore that Grimani would welcome him in Venice.

The banquet that Grimani ordered in Chigi's honor was sumptuous. Many fashionably dressed ladies were present, and it was attended by Venetian patricians of great prominence. Among them was Bernardo Bembo, in his youth a great friend of Lorenzo Magnifico and by now a Nestor-like figure in the Venetian councils, the councilors Piero Duodo, Giorgio Emo, and Luca Tron, the banker Alvise Pisani, and the brothers Lorenzo and Piero Cappello, who were closely connected with the great banking house of Cappello-Vendramin.[3] Grimani's banquet is remarkable for two reasons: first, because it took place at all; and then because of the role the guests had in Venetian politics. In taking a closer look at these two facts of Grimani's reception, we can make out a picture of the situation that existed in Venice in the early months of the year 1511, and we can understand better the sensation aroused by Chigi's appearance in Venice.

W HEN CHIGI arrived in Venice, the republic was in its second winter of war and was faced by steadily increasing difficulties that were building up to a crisis. The preceding months had been harsh for the inhabitants of the city. It was unusual at that time to carry on military operations beyond autumn, but at the insistence of Pope Julius II the campaign had been continued throughout the winter. The results were disappointing: most of the terra firma remained in the hands of the enemy. Thus, the hard campaign had created no improvement in the situation and, with spring approaching, Venice had to prepare itself for a French offensive from the west and a German attack from the north.

The inhabitants of the city were still living under the pressure that had developed two years earlier, when in 1509 the war broke out and the terra firma fell into enemy hands. Peasants fleeing from pillaging mercenaries had streamed into Venice.[4] They had been settled in monasteries such as San Giorgio, San Niccolò, and Sant' Andrea which the monks, evading the hardships of the war, had left empty. When the fighting abated, some peasants had gone back to their land, but others remained in the

17

city and in the spring of 1510, with enemy troops again pouring into the terra firma, more refugees arrived; some of them were housed in the empty Fondaco dei Tedeschi. A special group among the refugees settling in Venice were the Jews, who until the War of the League of Cambrai, had supported themselves as moneylenders to the poor on the terra firma and had not been permitted to enter Venice. Thievery, never unknown to Venice, increased with this influx of aliens and outsiders into the crowded space of the island city.

The life of these refugees was grim, and their presence in Venice was felt by the entire city: even without the sudden increase in population, the war had caused goods to be scarce and prices dear. The wealth of Venice, the richest city of early sixteenth-century Europe, came from trade, and Venetian trade suffered severely from the war.

Venice was under siege on land. The sea roads, however, were open. Although there was no particular reason why the regular convoys to the East, to Alexandria and Beirut, should not continue their usual schedules, there were impediments. Naval operations in the Po against Ferrara, and the needed imports of foodstuffs from the region along the Adriatic Sea, required ships and sailors. At the time of the sailing of the convoys in early spring, the seamen were not available and the galleys were not fully equipped. These delays made it necessary to issue legislation that would permit the captains to stay in Alexandria beyond their customary loading time. The date of the return of the convoys and of the arrival of goods became uncertain.[5]

The war also changed the nature of the trade between Venice and the East. Venice could still export some of its specialties: soap, glassware from Murano, and copperware, but other goods —silverware and cloth, for example—had to be exported in reduced amounts because the Venetian government needed the silver, and much of the cloth sold in the East had been manufactured in Germany or in now inaccessible parts of Italy.[6] On the other hand, Venice needed goods from the eastern Mediterra-

18

nean which the war situation required: saltpeter—for use in gunpowder—and foodstuffs, particularly grain. In contrast, the expensive items that had formed a good part of the cargos of the galleys on their return journeys and that had brought the greatest profits—spices, silk, precious stones—were less desirable because they were difficult to sell. Foreign merchants who usually gathered in Venice at the time of the return of the convoys from the East in late spring and late fall no longer came, and the roads on which goods had been sent for sale to other parts of Italy, Germany, or France were blocked or unsafe.

Venice's overland trade was not entirely cut off by the war, and the government tried to facilitate the import of wine and grain by lifting restrictions on foreign ships and merchants.[7] But this trade could not be maintained to any great extent or with regularity. Trade to the areas controlled by the French stopped entirely; a certain amount of traffic over the Alps continued. However, the relations of Venice with the Free Cities of southern Germany showed the difficulties to which commercial relations were subjected during the war.

At the beginning of the war, the Venetian government assured the Free Cities of Nuremberg, Ulm, Strassburg, and Augsburg that "Your merchants can trade, live and leave Venice and its dominion in security and can buy, keep and export their possessions and wares without being molested"; and it confirmed this promise in a solemn decree in April 1509.[8] But when Venice was placed under ban by the German imperial court, Emperor Maximilian, despite some hesitation and despite lengthy protestations from the governments of the Free Cities, ordered all trade with Venice suspended. He made exceptions, however: in January 1510 he gave the powerful Augsburg firm of Welser and Föhlen permission to transport a considerable load of cloth to Venice and to import goods from there. He assured them of protection on the roads. Maximilian continued to give various German merchants safe conduct for bringing goods to and from Venice. At the end of December, for example, we hear that there was great activity in the Fondaco dei Tedeschi.[9] German merchants had moved in, had bought pepper, ginger, and other spices and wares for large sums, and were now in a great rush to bale them and transport them to Germany. The safe conduct given by Maximilian was a requisite for these business transactions, but there was no guarantee that his orders would be observed. Tyrolian nobles who believed they had claims against Venice, and even the Duke of Bavaria, confiscated goods coming from Venice, and Maximilian himself wavered in his attitude. In the spring of 1511 he threatened to close all the passes from the north to the south; he then deferred enforcement, but carried through this threat two years later.

Venetians also could no longer rely on a regular supply of daily necessities, foodstuffs, and wine from the terra firma. Because of the war, the land was frequently left fallow or the armies confiscated what the farmers produced. Grain, cattle, and wine had to be brought from greater distances by ship and accordingly became more costly. For instance, grain prices doubled almost immediately upon the onset of the war and fluctuated with the amount that could be imported.

The rise of prices, especially of foodstuffs, was hard to bear because people had to live on diminishing incomes. With the outbreak of the war, the government had decreed that for six months all officials would receive no pay;[10] at the same time, they were prohibited from resigning or seeking other employment. Inspectors were appointed to make sure that the officials fulfilled their functions as before. The consequences of this decree were not as devastating as might appear at first glance, since the fees the officials received from those who needed their services were as important as their salaries. However, whereas before the war they could keep the fees in their entirety, they were now obligated to give 50 percent of their income from fees to the government. This economy measure concerned government officials of every kind, not only employees like scribes, clerks, and messengers but also the members of the ruling nobility who in the city or in the republic held positions that involved the receipt of fees. This decree was prolonged from six months to six months more, and remained in force throughout the entire war.

The effects of the decrease of Venetian trade were felt by many groups of the population and created unemployment in certain areas of economic life. When it appeared that the scheduled sailing of the convoys to Flanders and England would be impossible, thus bringing about an acute shortage of wool, which would in turn throw numerous Venetian cloth workers out of work, the government lifted the restrictions on the import of wool: during a determined period of time, Venetians and foreigners, by road or by ship from England, Flanders, or Barbary, could bring wool into Venice. The old law that Venetian ships must be used for goods to be sold in Venice was abrogated, thus permitting Venetians to bring in goods on foreign ships.[11]

Those hardest hit by the insecurity and the decline of trade were the small merchants. The economic importance of their wares was not great enough to arouse the interest of rulers who would intervene to assure safe transport; nor could they rely on imports from the terra firma. They were hurt by the absence of foreign merchants, by the lack of regularly held markets, and by the change in trade with the East. The journey eastward was no longer made by small ships but by convoys of galleys, and priority was given to goods needed for the war. By a fortunate accident the letters that one of these merchants of modest means, Martino Merlini, wrote to his brother who tried to do business in the East are preserved and give a lively picture of the difficulties the war had brought to this group of citizens.[12]

After half a year of the war, Merlini wrote: "One can think and talk of nothing but of war, plague and scarcity, but most of all about the war. The war makes us forget the plague because the time has come about which our forefathers said that the living will envy the dead."[13] At the end of December 1509, Merlini complains bitterly of how the general expensiveness had reduced the circumstances of life for him and his family: "For more than half of the week we must get along without meat, and I must confess that I mix water in the wine when the wine is still in the casket."[14] The picture that emerges from these letters is somewhat ambiguous. On one hand Merlini gives the impression that almost all possibilities of earning money by trade have ended. The roads are closed, and everyone thinks it is better to keep the goods he has than to sell them. Moreover, nobody wants to buy anything. Merlini wrote in another letter from the same year, 1509, that to talk now about trade makes as much sense as it would to discuss the possibility of trade in an uninhabited village. He advises his brother to stay in the East because in Venice a merchant has no chance. On the other hand Merlini loses no opportunity to attempt to enter what might be a promising transaction. He himself has little to offer, with the exception of glassware and soap. Silverware, which had been a very popular export, is no longer available because the government mints the silver. But there are certain things his brother might send because military requirements have increased their value. Merlini had some information about saltpeter mines in Tripoli and asks his brother to investigate them, since saltpeter is in high demand. It might also be possible to make great profits from material to be used in making sails, and special wares, such as medicinal herbs, might fetch good prices. People are still buying precious stones—rubies, diamonds, turquoise—but only very rich merchants can afford to trade in them.

There is no point, Merlini cautions, in sending to Venice goods that are not in particular demand, not only because it would be difficult to sell them but also because the entire profit would go into taxes. Whatever difficulties the war has created for the pursuit of trade, the most pernicious, the most ruinous, factor is taxes. Complaints about taxes occupy more and more space in Merlini's letters and become almost their main theme: "It seems to me if this damned war lasts for another year, we

22

shall have lost everything and be ruined because of what we have to pay for our food and then for what we have to pay in taxes." His desperation about the taxes he has to pay becomes obsessive—but Merlini had some reason for his worries. The taxes imposed between January and April 1511 were as numerous and high as the taxes that had been raised at the height of the crisis in 1509, and this even after the tax screw had been continuously applied in the intervening years.[15] Merlini was in the deepest gloom. His brother had sent to the children of the house a parrot and wrote to ask whether it had learned to speak. The answer he received is almost offensive: "Certainly the parrot is well but has not learned anything because we have other things on our minds than to teach a parrot to speak. What we have gone through in the last two years drives every kind of pleasure out of our heads."

Of course, there were groups among the Venetian population that suffered less from the war. Although the decline of imports created unemployment among certain groups, workers were in demand for shipbuilding, which thrived as a result of the war, and the products of other economic occupations, for instance, glass and soap, continued to be of use on the domestic market and for export. The rich upper group of the Venetian patriciate, although not unaffected by the war, did not experience the hardships that the rest of the population suffered. They lived on a grander scale than the average citizen. Merlini is well aware of this difference.[16] He is insistent that his brother carry out expeditiously some business he has undertaken for Pietro Diedo. Diedo is, according to Merlini, very rich, probably worth 20-30,000 ducats and, although still young, is already a member of the Council of Savi. Thus, a contact with him may make the brother's fortune. Merlini himself, desperate in early 1511 to make some kind of profit, thinks he might move himself and the entire family out into the country, where he can live on what he plants and get good prices for his products. He believes this might be possible because he has some contacts with a certain Contarini, who plans to lease a large piece of land and might give Merlini a share.

In Merlini's eyes, the economic position of the great Venetian families was barely impaired by the war. Indeed, although from the perspective of a troubled man their position might have appeared more impregnable than it really was, the income of many of these families did remain considerable during the war. Some had profitable investments in the Venetian dominions, in Crete or Cyprus. Either alone or with others they successfully bid for the use of galleys in the auctions before the sailing of convoys, and through their political activities and connections they had information as to which goods in wartime circumstances were in greatest demand. Their contacts with the military allowed them to bring agricultural products from their estates to the market in Venice. They could go on living in their accustomed style.

Luxurious living was liable to arouse resentment, especially since many members of the wealthy families were entrenched in the running of the government and the sufferings and misery of the rest of the population might appear to have been caused by the policies they had pursued. Even Sanudo, more inclined to admire the rich and powerful than to criticize them, showed some discontent when he heard that the ship in which Alvise Arimondo, the newly appointed ambassador to Constantinople, was to sail was held up at the Lido by unfavorable weather, and that while waiting for better weather, Arimondo had himself installed on Sant' Elena, an island that was virtually a part of Venice, drawing from the government his per diem allowance of five ducats.[17]

Venetians lived much too close to one another for the ruling group to remain unaware of the seething resentment. They took measures indicating that they feared the discontent of the people might take dangerous, violent forms. The carnival season offered special occasion for unpleasant incidents, and the Council of Ten decreed in the first days of February 1511 that this year it was forbidden to wear masks or disguises.[18] Although this might be an appropriate security measure, prohibition of pleasures that would be missed by everyone hardly served to lower the social tension. Thus, on February 14, 1511, a proposal that carried the names of the entire Collegio, meant to show that the government demanded sacrifices from all groups of the population, even from the upper group, was introduced in the Pregadi.[19] The preface of the proposal, which was accepted by an overwhelming majority, reveals its motives: "Although we are in great danger, as everyone knows, there are many who in disregard of God and of the obligations to Him and in disregard of the honor and the needs of our republic . . . continue to spend high, unnecessary sums of money. By this they do damage to themselves and cause general resentment; they show little love for their fatherland since many spend this money without having paid their taxes, which are imposed to preserve this state and to secure the existence of us all." The government proposed to appoint two officials, Procurators of San Marco, who would be responsible for enforcing laws designed to prevent unnecessary luxury and spending. These officials soon spelled out the rules to be enforced.[20] All ostentatious display was prohibited; dress must be simple, and the wearing of jewelry was forbidden.

A few days after these restrictions had been publicly announced, Antonio Grimani gave the banquet in honor of Chigi which was attended by twenty ladies elegantly dressed and bejeweled. This was an open infringement of the decree issued the week before. There had been quick protests when word of the banquet was circulating, and a prominent lawyer, Gasparo Malipiero, had asked the government to intervene and forbid the holding of the banquet.[21] Grimani had forestalled this move by obtaining special permission, although this did not satisfy those who advocated a strict interpretation of the law: Grimani had gone only to the Council of Ten to seek exception to the law and not to the Pregadi. It must be said here that not only Grimani but also others who attended his party—Bernardo Bembo, Pie-

25

tro Duodo, Giorgio Emo, Luca Tron, Lorenzo Cappello, Alvise Pisani—had sponsored the law against luxury in the Pregadi. They must have been aware of the impression that would be made if those who had introduced the law felt themselves not bound by it. The fact that Grimani insisted on giving his party and that the others were willing to attend it shows that they must have thought Chigi's presence had other purposes beyond the prosecution of a fraudulent debtor, that Chigi's visit might be of general importance for Venetian politics.

This becomes clear when we consider now the people who attended Grimani's party. As might be expected, they were high in the government, but some men stand out: Alvise Pisani and the brothers Lorenzo and Piero Cappello. The names Pisani and Cappello occur frequently in the documents of the time not only as members of the Council of Savi, to which they belonged almost uninterruptedly,[22] but as financiers deeply involved in the hiring and maintenance of the armed forces. Bankers had a crucial role in war financing, but the number of banks in Venice was small. At the time of the outbreak of the War of the League of Cambrai, there were only three banking houses in Venice: that of Alvise Pisani, that of Cappello-Vendramin, and that of the diarist Girolamo Priuli. The campaigns of 1510 and their continuation throughout the winter had placed an increasing, dangerous strain on their resources.

When at the end of the year 1508 war had become a real and immediate threat, the Pregadi discussed in several meetings the size of the military forces they needed to put into the field and how to finance this army.[23] The sum needed to conduct a campaign for a single year, beginning in spring and lasting throughout the summer, was calculated to amount to 240,000 ducats. Of this sum, 100,000 ducats cannot be regarded as an emergency outlay because they were for the commanders of the towns, islands, and fortresses in the Venetian empire along the Adriatic Coast down to Greece. The remaining 140,000 ducats were for the condottieri taken into service for the impending war. The commander-in-chief—captain-general was his title—was Niccolo Orsini, Count of Pitigliano; he received a yearly salary of 50,000 ducats. The second in command, with the title governor-general, was Bartolommeo d'Alviano; he received 30,000 ducats.[24] Next to them, a large number of other condottieri, with much smaller salaries, were taken into service by the Venetians; the contract also established how many men each of the condottiere had to provide.[25]

Although nobody doubted the need for hiring the services of Orsini and d'Alviano, the extraordinary size of this military budget aroused some debate. The money to defray the military expenses was to come from the towns of the terra firma—Padua, Vicenza, Verona, Brescia, Bergamo, Cremona, Crema, Udine, Treviso, Rovigo, Ravenna, Rimini, and Fiume—but the revenues they could normally provide would not be sufficient. So additional taxes were imposed on these towns. When the towns of the terra firma fell to the enemy after the beginning of military operations, the consequence was not only the loss of numerous lucrative administrative positions for the members of the Venetian nobility, and a diminution of trade that reduced the earnings of the merchants and the income from duties to be paid to the Venetian government; it also forced the government to seek new revenues in order to finance the war.[26]

The government took the same recourse that all governments apply in similar situations: it increased taxes.[27] With the loss of the revenues from the terra firma, the Venetian government had to rely on taxes that were paid by the inhabitants of the city. The indirect taxes—duties on consumer goods, such as wine and oil, and the revenue derived from the administration of the salt monopoly—could not be greatly increased; indeed, the income from these sources fell off as a result of the recession caused by the war. The only taxes that could be more fully exploited were direct taxes. They had been introduced in the middle of the fifteenth century; every inhabitant of Venice had been obligated to register the value of his houses and other immovable possessions in Venice and on the terra firma, as well as the rents he received from his property. On the basis of these registers a tax was raised called the *decima* because it imposed the payment of one tenth of the income from the registered possessions. In quiet times, this tax was imposed twice during one year, but in the first war year of 1509, the decima was levied nine times; in 1510 and 1511 five and six times. It ought to be added that only a part of the decima was a direct tax in the modern sense, meaning payment of a sum without expectation of repayment or compensation; this part of the decima was called *decima persa* (lost decima). But another part of the decima was treated as a loan on which the government had to pay interest, usually 5 percent, and which it was expected to repay after a certain number of years.

The institution that administered the money loaned to the government was called the Monte, and to it, as security, the income from certain taxes was assigned; people could sell their claims to portions of the Monte. In economically prosperous times, rights to capital in the Monte—we would say, to shares of the Monte—had a good value, and many Venetians invested their money this way. In times of war and economic difficulties, the government was unable to keep up the promised repayment schedule and frequently stopped paying interest altogether. Then the value of the Monte shares fell, and they became almost worthless. After the loss of the terra firma, and under the financial pressure of the war, the Monte was no longer able to make any payments; its insolvency added to the economic difficulties of many Venetians. However, the writing-off of the debts that the government owed to those who had paid their taxes or part of their taxes as loans did not mean that the system of taxation was changed. The assumption remained that part of the decima was a loan, and, in November 1509, a new Monte, called Monte Novissimo, was established: it was expected to pay interest on the tax-loans deriving from the wartime taxes and finally to repay them.

The establishment of the Monte Novissimo was needed for a

further urgent reason. In addition to tightening the tax screws, Venice—like other Renaissance governments—had another method of raising money in emergency situations: voluntary loans, which the wealthier citizens were expected, almost forced, to contribute. These loans, too, were inscribed on the Monte and were supposed to produce interest and to be repaid. The issue of the loans became particularly pressing in 1510. The Doge Loredan appealed to the members of the Pregadi from bench to bench. But it was a sign of the loss of confidence in Venice's chances of recovering its financial strength that these appeals, particularly the later ones, brought disappointingly small sums into the chests of the treasury.

Venice's financial difficulties were augmented by a misguided approach to the financing of its military efforts. Like governments of other, more recent times, the Venetians did not expect the war to last long and calculated that, if they would overcome the present emergency, the future would take care of itself. Furthermore, they needed cash very urgently and placed a premium on receiving money quickly. Those who paid their taxes before a certain date, or supplied the promised loans quickly, would be credited at the Monte for an amount larger than what they actually paid. Moreover, they could use their shares in the Monte as payment on future taxes. By agreeing to accept these assignations, the government diminished its income from future taxes. So in overcoming the present emergency, the problems of the future were aggravated.

Another reason for a decrease in government income was inherent in the nature of a mercenary army. Unavoidably, a gap occurred between the date when payments to the army had to be made and the time when the money from taxes raised for this purpose was available. This is where the services of the bankers were indispensable; they bridged the gap by making advances to the government. They demanded greater security than taxes or loans that had not yet even been agreed upon and were prospects rather than certainty. And, therefore, the bankers received

claims on government revenues such as the salt tax, from which
regular returns could be expected, but again with the result that
even income from these sources became mortgaged for months
ahead. The length of the war and the seriousness of the situation
which had arisen from the advance of the enemies into the terra
firma forced the Venetian rulers to go beyond the traditional
methods of war financing and to invent new devices.

In March 1510 a process began which lasted throughout the
war on an ever-enlarging scale: the sale of offices.[28] At first,
minor jobs and small businesses that the government farmed out
for a determined number of years were offered for lifetime or
even for hereditary possession to those who held them and were
willing to pay a certain amount of money. Soon afterwards, on
March 17, the Council of Ten decided that on payment of 2000
ducats each, ten nobles could become members of the Pregadi
for one year, but without the right to vote. Of these 2000 ducats
1000 would be credited to them on the Monte, and with the receipt for the other 1000 ducats they would be permitted to pay
their future taxes. The number of ten nobles admitted on the
basis of such a financial contribution was soon raised, and by
the beginning of the winter of 1510-11, thirty-nine nobles had
entered the Pregadi in this way. But in September the price for
admission to the Pregadi had come down to 1000 ducats; moreover, the money could be paid in installments, and those who
paid the sum remained members not just for one year but until
the government had repaid the loan. By allowing the rich nobles
to buy themselves into the Pregadi, the government took in
around 40,000 ducats, but the attractiveness of this opportunity
declined in proportion to the increase in the number of those
who availed themselves of it.

In the fall of 1510 sources for financing the war were running
dry, and the Pope's insistence that a campaign against Ferrara
ought to be mounted in the winter aggravated the precarious
financial situation. From the two provveditori, Andrea Gritti,
with one part of the army at Montanara to protect Venice against

attack from the north, and Paolo Cappello with the other half, cooperating with papal troops, came desperate requests for money which the Venetian government was able to meet only with great difficulty.[29] The campaign against Ferrara, because of its bearing on Venice's relations with the Pope and on maintaining his goodwill, was considered particularly important, and Cappello's requests enjoyed a certain preference. Thus, to the pleased astonishment of the Pregadi, Cappello told the government on October 27 what no provedditore had ever written them before: he had enough money.[30] Gritti, however, received less and his needs were not satisfied. He apologized about having to demand money in each of his reports, but "God knows that I don't write your Highness because I do not appreciate the anxiety or the effort involved but only because at the present moment it seems to me necessary that my troops ought to be as satisfied as your other troops who have been paid."[31] The two provedditori, Gritti and Cappello, were aware that lack of success did not strengthen the popularity of their demands for money. When an attack of his troops against Verona got bogged down in tempestuous rains, Gritti was anxious to emphasize as extenuating circumstances that "against the will of God one cannot advance."[32]

Because of the scarcity of money, delays in payment, and military failures, the situation reached a crisis point in the early months of 1511. The dangers for Venice came from two sides. The inhabitants of the terra firma were becoming increasingly hostile because they felt that they were badly treated, their interests disregarded. The soldiers without the pay due them lived from the land, plundering, looting, and using violence against the peasants who tried to fend them off. Gritti's reports describe what the population had to suffer. From all the surrounding villages peasants came to him who were beaten and injured and who had their furniture, wine, grain, cattle, clothes, all their goods, taken from them "by our soldiers."[33] He tells about a poor cattle merchant who with great effort had succeeded in bringing cattle of good quality from Parma into the Veneto in order to sell them in Venice. When he passed by a group of soldiers they took away his cattle, and he was now a ruined man. He could not stop crying and Gritti himself was moved; but no money was available to give this poor man even a small compensation.[34] In reporting these incidents Gritti was not inspired purely by sympathy or sentiment. He wanted the Venetian rulers to realize that the dissatisfaction which such outrages created turned the sympathies of the population away from Venice and "endangered our own interests."

But there was another danger in the fact that the soldiers had to take recourse to looting. Discipline fell apart, and the chances of resistance when the war heated up again seemed very questionable. In the middle of December, Gritti received 3000 ducats. In distributing the money to the commanders of six companies that had been without pay for two months, Gritti told them that this was an opportunity to restore discipline.[35] They ought to tell their men that they had to remain within camp, that they had to be orderly, that they could have no women in camp, and that violators would be severely punished. But such orders and appeals had no lasting effect because soon again payments failed to arrive. At the end of January Gritti reported that because the soldiers had to live from the land they were widely dispersed and could not be called quickly into action; the peasants continued to suffer. From then on the situation steadily deteriorated. Not only Gritti but also Cappello began to raise more urgent demands for money. They were almost frantic because it was becoming evident that the French were assembling troops for an offensive; the provveditori feared that their discontented and badly disciplined troops were no match for them. Moreover, some of the condottieri used this as an occasion to announce that, if they did not receive the promised money, they no longer felt bound to their agreements and might simply march off.[36] The climax came on March 21, 1511, when a report from Cappello arrived according to which the French were steadily getting

reinforcements, whereas the Venetian troops and their condottieri, disaffected by the delays in pay, did not want to put up a
fight. The rulers of Venice could no longer doubt that the situation was not only extremely serious but that it was necessary to
take action with great speed.[37]

Throughout the preceding months, the Venetian patricians
who determined policy were aware of the needs of the army but
had been inclined to think that the provveditori, in order to be
heard, had painted in exaggeratedly dark colors the difficulties
of their situation. Probably like other bankers, Priuli reacted
with great suspicion when he heard these incessant demands for
money. His diary has entries in which—clearly in some exasper-
ation—he notes that, as usual, the two provveditori are still at
the same place where they had been before, that they were doing
nothing, were losing time, and the only thing they did was to
shout, "Money, money."[38] But during March the mood changed.
The government became aware that the French offensive threatened the existence of the Venetian Republic and that resistance to
the French would be possible only if the requests of the provveditori were filled. The extent to which the Venetian rulers felt
threatened emerges from a long reflection which, still in the first
week of March, Priuli set down. It is worth citing at length because it deals not only with the difficulties of the present, but
also summarizes the factors that had brought about this situation.[39]

The main issue, Priuli said, was the lack of financial resources.
In previous times, the terra firma and Lombardy were the areas
that had provided almost all the money for maintaining a military force. Now the entire burden was falling on the inhabitants
of Venice, but providing money for an army was like drying out
an ocean. The taxes were no longer bearable, especially because
of the lack of trade and work. As long as people earned money,
they were willing to pay taxes in order to preserve their precious
liberty and so as not to fall into the hands of enemies from the
other side of the Alps. Money for the soldiers had to be found,

but payments were delayed, and when the soldiers had been told they would receive payments in the course of forty-five days and after fifty days had received nothing, only promises, they looted the land; then the peasants had to be supported lest they die of hunger. And large companies of soldiers simply left the camp. This was particularly dangerous because the Pope could draw the conclusion that the Venetians were unwilling to make the sacrifices necessary for the conduct of the war; he might come to an understanding with France. On the other hand, when the French became aware that the Venetians were unable to keep up their army, they would be encouraged to pursue their offensive more energetically. At the end of these reflections, Priuli embarks on an attack against Gritti; he writes that he is aware that Gritti enjoys a great reputation all over Italy, but he does poor service in the present situation because, with his prognostications of complete ruin without the money he is asking for, he is driving the senators to desperation. Priuli was present when Gritti's reports were read in the Senate, and he says he is now reluctant to attend sessions because he gets depressed over all the lamentations and complaints.

Yet, with the arrival of Cappello's report on March 21 when the crisis was at its height, Priuli played a prominent role in overcoming it. The Venetian patrician who then served as controller, supervising the flow of government money, was Lorenzo Priuli, Girolamo Priuli's father. Girolamo, as he notes in his diary, felt that he could not refuse his revered father, and that very night Girolamo managed to lay his hands on 3000 ducats, which he brought to the controller's office so that they could be sent immediately to Cappello.

Priuli's report provides a dramatic account of the role of the Venetian bankers in this war. As far as conclusions can be drawn from our somewhat spotty documentary material, all payments the two provveditori, Gritti and Cappello, had received since the beginning of 1511 were loans advanced by the Venetian banking houses.[40] During March alone 13,500 ducats were sent to Cappello; 8000 of them were lent by the Cappello-Vendramin; 5500 by Girolamo Priuli as head of the Priuli bank. Because imposition of further decime or appeals for forced loans did not promise to bring in significant amounts, those sources were no longer regarded as guaranteeing repayment of the advances made by the bankers. Therefore, the bankers asked for and received other securities: assignation of the tax on the Jews, on the duties on export of wine and oil, and on the salt tax. But since the income from these taxes was limited, not one but several creditors received assignations of the same source of revenue. Cappello-Vendramin would have to wait until Priuli's claims had been satisfied by revenues from the wine tax; for another loan Priuli would have to wait until the Procurators of San Marco had received their loan back from the salt tax. It is no wonder that Priuli, when he described his efforts to assist his father, remarked that he regretted having become a banker because he now suspected that it might finish badly and he might go bankrupt, along with many other bankers. The bankers had always played an essential role in the payment mechanism, bridging the time gap between the need for immediate cash and the influx of cash from decime and forced loans. But by the beginning of the spring of 1511, the time gap between the need for immediate cash and the influx of cash from decime and loans widened enormously. Involvement in government finances began to place a heavy strain on the resources of the bankers; the dates for the repayment of their advances grew longer and longer.

At the same time, the need for money was still great. The spring would certainly bring an increase in military activities. The Pope would demand from the Venetians a strenuous military effort, and Venice had much reason to be concerned about remaining on good terms with Julius II. The Pope had the possibility of coming to an understanding with the French which Venice did not have.[41] Moreover, the Pope was trying to persuade the German king to abandon his alliance with France, and the

Venetians feared that Maximilian's change of front might be attained at the expense of Venice: either by promising Maximilian a good part of the Venetian terra firma, or by asking the Venetians to pay Maximilian a high tribute for their possessions. Finally, both the Pope and the Venetians were convinced that, in the war against France, intervention of the Swiss Landsknechte might be decisive—the Swiss placed a high price on their services. The need for money dominated the thinking of the Venetian ruling group as the third campaign of the War of the League of Cambrai was about to start. The arrival of a man who was reputed to be the richest merchant of the world would have aroused curiosity among the Venetian population in any circumstances; but in the straitened circumstances brought about by the war, limitless wealth commanded particular awe and curiosity. But, clearly, his presence was of special interest to the wealthy and the bankers. It was unavoidable that from the outset there was much speculation about Chigi's real purposes in coming to Venice.

--⋯⊰{ III }⊱⋯--

The Contract

ON MARCH 2, 1511, some light was thrown on Chigi's intentions when it was rumored that he was discussing with the Venetian government a deal that would involve the sale of a great amount of alum and a considerable sum of cash.[1] Alum is a mineral salt needed at that time for binding dyes to cloth, and it was also used in glass manufacturing. In the middle of the fifteenth century, rich veins of alum were discovered at Tolfa, about 70 kilometers north of Rome. The popes saw in this discovery a sign from God, for the Tolfa lode more than supplied Christendom's need for alum, which previously had come from Asia Minor, now under the domination of the infidel Turk. Thus the popes took the exploitation of the Tolfa mines into their own hands, proclaiming that all Christians ought to satisfy their needs for alum from Tolfa and that the revenues from this be used to finance the struggle against the infidels.[2]

Chigi had farmed the Tolfa mines for the Curia, and he had a particular interest in the Venetian market because Venice was the port through which alum from other mines, namely, the Turkish mines in Asia Minor, could—and did—enter the European market. Chigi had an obvious interest in forcing the Venetians to observe the monopoly of the papal alum mines. Three weeks after rumors about a deal between Chigi and the Venetian government had first been heard, the negotiations had already reached the point that Chigi, together with the heads of the Council of Ten, appeared before the Doge and the Collegio in order to explain the projected bargain, according to which Chigi would provide alum and a cash sum and Venice would give him security.[3] The negotiations seemed almost concluded, but more than three weeks pass before we hear more about this business.

A catastrophic event occurred in Venice at this time, which provides the explanation. On March 26, 1511, Venice was hit by a devastating earthquake and tremors continued over the following days.[4] With the moving of the ground, all the bells in Venice's church towers began to ring simultaneously and then, dislocated, they fell silent—both equally terrifying events in Venice where, almost always above the din of the town, bells can be heard indicating the time of day or the canonical hours. The water surged up in the canals, and the people fled in boats to get away from buildings threatening to collapse. Some statues from the facade of San Marco and the ducal palace fell, and people saw in their ruin both good and bad omens. That some sculptured lilies had been smashed was believed to indicate that the King of France, who had the lily as an emblem, would be driven out of Italy; to others, the destruction of the statue of Prudence was taken as a warning that in the future the rulers of Venice ought to show more care than they had in recent years. The Venetians were powerfully reminded that there were forces over which they had no control. This gave the priests an occasion to demonstrate their importance. The recently appointed patriarch, Antonio Contarini, appeared in the Pregadi and explained that the disaster was a sign of God, who had punished the Venetians for their sins. He accused Venice of being a thoroughly amoral city. Nunneries served the sexual needs of the rich and powerful. Homosexuality was so widespread that female prostitutes had come to him complaining that they earned so little they had to exercise their profession into old age. When anyone was accused of such crimes, the magistrates closed their eyes and ears because they themselves behaved in the same way. People no longer came to confession; whereas in previous years in the midst of Lent half of the population went to confession, this year chiefly pious old women and only a few others had appeared. The patriarch ordered, therefore, that all ought to fast for three days, consuming only bread and water, and that every evening in all the squares of Venice the priests should lead their parishioners in processions, chanting litanies and imploring God's forgiveness.

This appeal to Christian piety had—at least momentarily—a strong impact because behind all the pride in Venice's power and wealth, a disquiet feeling had grown up about the contrast between Venetian luxury and the doctrines of Christianity. Not just the people, even some philosophically minded younger patricians, were having serious doubts about the behavior of Venetian society. In the winter of 1510-11 Pietro Giustiniani and Vincenzo Quirini, members of Venice's oldest and most respected families, renounced promising political careers to become monks.[5] The notions of the patriarch certainly corresponded to what most of the people were thinking, for great crowds participated in the processions, the churches were full, and many went to confession. The actions of the government reflected this atmosphere of religious fervor.[6] On March 27, the government reinforced the legislation against homosexuality; and although it gave some protection to the Jews when fanatic preachers turned the people against them, declaring that God's ire had been aroused because Venice had permitted Jews to mix among Christians, the government commanded the Jews to leave Venice within a month and until then to stay in their houses; they were permitted to come out only for two hours in the morning and two hours in the afternoon.

Marino Sanudo found the measures of the patriarch and the government most praiseworthy insofar as their possible effects on morals and religiosity were concerned. But he considered them valueless as a remedy against a natural phenomenon like an earthquake.[7] Sanudo's attitude probably reflected the views of many members of the Venetian upper class, and it must be said—not unlike the strong but short-lived effects that the appeals of great preachers had on the urban populations of late-medieval Europe—that life in Venice after a few days of religious fervor and penitence soon returned to its regular course.

When the discussion with Chigi was resumed, the question of the compatibility of the contract with the prescripts of the Church was for many a serious obstacle to the agreement. For this reason, the earthquake takes its place in the history of Chigi's loan. Before the earthquake, the agreement was almost completed; indeed, two weeks after the catastrophe, on April 15, a proposal very much like the one later adopted was presented.[8] Yet the doubts this contract aroused were so strong that it took more than a month until a conclusion was reached.

The contract that one of the Savi, Alvise da Molin, outlined to the Pregadi on April 15 comprised a number of interconnected arrangements. Chigi would sell alum to the Venetian government for a large sum of ducats; he also would advance a loan of 40,000 ducats in two installments. Chigi requested securities for this loan: they were to consist of jewelry and solemn promises that some leading Venetian citizens would pledge their own money for the repayment of the loan. On the other hand, the government would not have to worry about selling the alum because another merchant was already willing to commit himself to buy it. Sanudo, whose diary gives this information, provides only a bare outline of the projected contract and does not fully reveal what the benefits of this bargain for the two contracting parties were or why the contract met some vehement objections in Venice. But information about the later course of the negotiations gives an answer to these questions.

For the Venetians the contract with Chigi had the advantage that a great amount of cash would be immediately at their disposal. Not only would they receive a loan from Chigi, but they would have additional amounts of money in hand because they would have to begin to pay for the alum they bought from Chigi only in 1513; the merchant who bought the alum from the Venetians would have to begin his payments to the Venetians immediately. Chigi received important concessions in exchange: the government guaranteed that no other alum would be permitted to appear on the Venetian market, and it allowed Chigi to set the price for the alum sold in Venice. This particular issue was of great interest to Chigi: the merchant who was to buy the alum from the Venetian government was Alessandro Schiapi, an employee of Chigi's; the price he would pay for the alum was lower, of course, than the price that the Venetian government paid Chigi for the same alum. In other words, this was a fictitious sale, meant to conceal the fact that, contrary to the laws of the Church against usury, Venice was paying high interest for money received as a loan. The advantages Chigi drew from this deal are clear: he made sure of his alum monopoly in the Venetian market; he could sell alum there at a high price and received pledges and securities that made certain the repayment of the money he advanced; finally, he received a good amount of interest on his loan. These were far-reaching concessions from which the Venetian government gained only one, but very great, advantage: the financial pressure would be eased for quite some time.

It was so evident that the contract had both advantages and disadvantages that its conclusion necessarily encountered heavy opposition.[9] The opponents had two chief arguments. In their view it was obvious that first the acquisition and then the sale of the alum represented a circumvention of the prohibition against usury, and nothing good could come from a measure that violated God's laws. In this context the opponents of the contract also found some justification for their attitude in a clause on which Chigi insisted—all litigation must be decided in Rome before the Rota. This meant that Chigi could attempt to enforce the execution of the contract with spiritual weapons. Thus the contract was raised beyond the level of pragmatic considerations; it could become a burden on the conscience of the Venetians.

The other powerful argument of the opponents of the contract was that it would be a serious blow to the prestige of the Venetian Republic. Venice had always been considered a city of inexhaustible wealth. If it now became known that the Venetian government had turned to a non-Venetian banker for financial assistance, it would be generally assumed that Venice was in desperate straits. Even those who might be willing to help might abandon Venice as a hopeless cause; it ought to be kept in mind, Priuli says, "that governments, rulers and republics rule and are maintained by what is believed about them rather than by correct evaluation of the situation." For this reason, Chigi's demand for jewels from the treasury of San Marco as security was considered to be particularly injurious. Behind the arguments of all the opponents there was the fundamental feeling that rejection of this kind of foreign help was a question of pride—a pride that had remained unbroken throughout all the defeats and catastrophes of recent years.

The advocates of the contract regarded arguments arising from moral scruples or traditional patriotic arrogance as inappropriate in the present emergency situation. There was one paramount consideration: "We must maintain the state and the republic." And Chigi's money was necessary for this purpose. Of course, the defenders of the contract also had answers to the objections. Although Chigi wanted to have pledges from individual rich Venetians, they all were part of the Venetian government. If Chigi accused them of failure to fulfill their obligations, they would not be prosecuted by the government, and since they were acting in accord with the government, excommunication or interdict should be of no particular concern to them. Moreover, Chigi had a reputation as a merchant of great reliability, and it was unlikely that he would sell the jewels from San Marco before they could be redeemed. Priuli calls the contract "shameful and dishonest," but "when you are in a storm and your ship is in danger of being wrecked, sailors won't bother about the ownership of the ship or of the goods the ship carries; without any other thought they will follow their natural instincts in order not to be drowned."

But the conflict over the agreement with Chigi involved not only contrasting views about the impact of the arrangement on Venice's political prospects; it was also exacerbated by rivalries among the ruling group and part of a power struggle among Venetian political leaders. What was happening during the months when the accord with Chigi hung fire gives us an opportunity to look below the smooth surface of Venetian politics and to get a view of the underlying factional struggles, despite the strictures on the formation of parties or blocs. We can also see how internal struggles affected the relationships among the various policymaking councils and magistracies.

It was natural that protagonists of the arrangement with Chigi would be those Venetian nobles who had close contacts in Rome and at the Curia.[10] The most eminent were the two Procurators of San Marco, Antonio Grimani and Giorgio Corner; both had sons who were cardinals and who had been helpful in smoothing the way for Venice's reconciliation with Pope Julius II. The policy of Grimani and Corner was directed to make close cooperation with the Pope the cornerstone of Venetian policy. Similar views were held by the Procurators Domenico Trevisan and Giorgio Emo, and by Alvise da Molin, Pietro Balbi, and Pietro Duodo. By serving as adjunct Savi during the interval after their term as Savi had ended and before they were eligible again, these men were almost continuously members of the Savi. Grimani served uninterruptedly after his return from exile in 1509; Pietro Balbi and Alvise da Molin uninterruptedly from 1510 to 1512, and Domenico Trevisan, Giorgio Emo, and Giorgio Corner, although somewhat less continuously, also for most of these years. Piero Duodo alternated between Counselor and Savio.[11]

Loosening the hold of this group over the Savi was a prerequisite for pursuing a different political course. Still, the pro-Pope policy was not popular in Venice. The conditions the Pope had imposed on Venice had left bitter feelings, and there was much criticism of the handling of affairs. The leader of this opposition was another Procurator, Antonio Tron, who from the end of the fifteenth century on had served in all the highest offices of the republic; from his family a recent Doge had come. There was a highly personal element in the hostility between

43

Grimani and Tron. In 1500, during the sensational trial that had resulted in Grimani's exile because of the defeat the Venetian fleet had suffered under his leadership, Tron had played an active role in urging Grimani's condemnation.[12] The two men could not have forgotten the bitter confrontation of the previous decade. In any case, soon after Grimani had returned from exile in 1509, he entered the Council of Savi and became a dominant figure.[13] Tron's influence declined and his criticisms of the Venetian ruling group became increasingly bitter.[14]

It would not be justified, however, to regard Tron's opposition as exclusively inspired by personal motives. His views had what we might call a philosophical basis, and we could apply to him the modern term "conservative." He insisted on rigid observation of established laws and rules; he was a proud patriot; he had been in favor of defending the areas of the Romagna, the occupation of which, after the fall of Cesare Borgia, had aroused the enmity of Julius II. When after Agnadello, two leading patricians, Giorgio Emo and Paolo Cappello, refused to accept election as provveditori with the army, Tron volunteered his services.[15] He objected strongly to the notion that the situation was so desperate that it was necessary to get assistance from the Turks,[16] and he regarded the Doge Lorenzo Loredan as discouragingly weak. He believed that a more energetic leadership could change the military situation. This was an attitude that found a clear echo among the large number of poor Venetian nobles who wanted to be relieved as quickly as possible of the financial burdens of the war—to enjoy again the fruits of the administrative positions on the terra firma. Among large groups of the Venetian nobility Tron was popular, and he was elected regularly to important positions.

There were many occasions, therefore, where the hostility between Tron and Grimani came out into the open. Most of them were concerned with practical issues, arising out of the needs of a diplomatic, military, or financial situation. For instance, when in January 1510 Tron failed to prevent the adoption of a financial measure that he considered adverse to the interests and rights of the Procurators of San Marco and the Scuole Grandi (fraternities of artisans), Tron threatened to stop coming to the Collegio or serving as Savio Grande. It was even rumored that he had said: "Nothing will be right in this city as long as this Doge rules."[17]

Yet because of Tron's basic conservatism, the conflict extended beyond disputes over concrete measures. He believed that the republic was being corrupted; government positions— the "benefits" and "honors" at the government's disposal—were not available to all Venetian nobles, as they ought to be, but were increasingly limited to a clique among them. A sign of the departure from the traditional principles of Venetian politics was the decline of the influence of the Great Council in relation to the Senate, as well as the surrender of power by the senate to a small group that dominated the Savi. Tron's opposition to Grimani and his group was particularly centered on this last issue.

When, in the critical months after the defeat of Agnadello, in July 1509 the Collegio proposed to the Pregadi the addition of three Savi for three months, the great importance Tron attributed to the composition of the Savi became evident.[18] The Collegio justified its request by pointing to the seriousness, the urgency, and the quantity of the decisions the Savi had to make in wartime; they were overburdened with work. The adjunct Savi should be free from the usual prohibition of having to wait as long as they had previously served before they could be re-elected; they could be elected to the Savi immediately after their term as adjunct Savio was over, and it was clearly expected that this would happen. Tron was elected an adjunct Savio, but he refused to take his seat. This enlargement of the Council of Savi seemed to him, as a strict defender of constitutional traditions, intolerable. He was willing to serve and continued to serve in the Council when he was elected on a regular basis, but not as an adjunct Savi. The conflict remained alive because requests for adjunct Savi were regularly renewed; and it came to a sharp explosion in July 1511, when the request was presented in somewhat modified form.

What happened in July 1511 was not only the renewal of the proposal that had been made successfully several times in the preceding years, to add three temporary members to the Council of Savi. This new proposal contained a special clause that invalidated previous legislation according to which no more than two Procurators of San Marco were permitted to be in the Council of Savi. It was suggested that there ought to be no restriction on the number of Procurators in the Council, and the rule that the Procurators who were elected to the Savi ought to be concerned with different parts of the city—either "de supra" or "de ultra" or "de citra"—was to be abolished. Antonio Grimani, Domenico Trevisan, and Giorgio Corner all were Procurators of San Marco.[19] They had completed their terms as regular Savio or adjunct Savio and were to leave the Council of Savi the following month. Clearly the intention of lifting the usual prohibitions was to get two of them, or perhaps all three, back into the Council. The vote in favor of this proposal in the Pregadi was not overwhelming—116 against 63. Moreover, because this suggestion was contradictory to previous legislation, it had to be approved not only by the Pregadi but also by the Great Council. When the meeting of the Great Council took place on July 13, Antonio Tron, who had been absent from the meeting of the Pregadi, made an appearance. This was a startling event because for many years—"in our time," as Sanudo wrote—no Procurator of San Marco had ever attended a meeting of the Great Council. It was assumed that Tron would get up and speak against the proposal, and under these circumstances the government did not dare to put the proposal to a vote. The proposal was dropped.[20]

After the notion of lifting the restrictions placed on the election of Procurators had been abandoned, the Pregadi went ahead in the usual manner and elected three additional Savi. With Domenico Trevisan and Antonio Grimani ineligible, two of their close collaborators, Pietro Balbi and Giorgio Emo, were elected. But the third newly elected member was Antonio Tron, and this time he accepted and joined the Council of Savi. In Sanudo's opinion, this was a mistake: Tron "did wrong."[21] But Sanudo overlooked the fact that Tron's action was not only inspired by concern with the maintenance of traditional customs; he wanted to prevent the monopoly of power by a small, closed group and might have believed he had a better chance to attain this goal from within the Collegio than from outside. Actually, together with Zaccaria Dolfin, a highly respected patrician with an outlook similar to his own, Tron tried to consolidate the success, which he had in July, by submitting in September a proposal that reinforced the rule that only two Procurators, and those from different sides of the Grand Canal, could be members of the Council of Savi. Moreover, the proposal stated that no Savio, after his term of six months had ended, could be reelected to the Council of Savi before six months had passed; this was meant to prevent an additional Savio from staying on for another six months in the Council as a regular member after his term had expired or to make it impossible for the regular member to remain in the Council as an adjunct. Membership in the Council of Savi would circulate more widely. The proposal of Tron and Delfin was accepted, but its effect was nullified because a clause was added that these regulations should not come into force during the current war.[22]

Probably the different outcomes of Tron's initiatives—his success in July, his failure in September—were related to the changing fortunes of war. In July, Julius II seemed to waver about continuing the war against France; the effectiveness of a pro-Pope policy on the part of Venice could be doubted. In September the conclusion of a holy league between the Pope, Spain, England, and Venice, which seemed to tilt the balance against France, was imminent. We shall look at these developments later in detail; with the description of the internal tensions in Venice and of Tron's opposition to the dominant politicians, we have gone chronologically far beyond April, when the agreement with

47

Chigi first took shape. But this digression seems appropriate because the tensions in Venice form the background of the negotiations with Chigi. These contrasts explain the strength of the resistance to the contract, the caution with which its advocates proceeded, and the length of time needed before a conclusion was reached.

From the time that Alvise da Molin outlined the main features of the contract with Chigi on April 15 to its adoption by the Pregadi, more than a month passed. Molin gave a more detailed report on April 23; the contract was read to the Pregadi, and it was decided that it deserved wider discussion.[23] However, enthusiasm for coming to a quick decision seems to have been small. At least on April 27, when a proposal for new taxes impressed upon the members of the Pregadi the gravity of the financial situation, Giorgio Emo used this as an opportunity to remind the Pregadi of the need to conclude the contract with Chigi.[24] This became more obvious when the taxes, now due, came in so slowly that, on May 7, the deadlines for their payment had to be prolonged.[25] The Council of Savi, therefore, submitted to the Pregadi a resolution in which it was said that a contract on the sale of alum, which promised to provide the government with a considerable amount of money, had been drawn up; it was suggested that three men be appointed—one Counselor, one Savio Grande, and one Savio di Terra Firma—to settle the final details with the other contracting party. Three days later, on May 10, these three negotiators and the other members of the Collegio should present their views about the contract to the Pregadi so that a final decision could be made. This proposal was accepted. Pietro Duodo as Counselor, Giorgio Corner as Savio Grande, and Pietro Lando as Savio di Terra Firma were elected to negotiate the details of the contract.[26]

As arranged, the Pregadi met on Saturday, May 10, and the contract in the form that now had been established was read to them; but since the Savi themselves were divided in their views, it was decided to take up the matter again two days later.[27] The reports about this meeting, held on May 12, explain why there was hesitation and division of opinion even among the Savi.[28] This question was raised: If the Venetian government bought such a great amount of alum, could it do better than to sell it with loss to Chigi's employee, Alessandro Schiapi? That is, could not the Venetian government itself sell the alum in the market? Gasparo Malipiero, who in February had raised objections to the luxury with which Grimani had honored the arrival of Chigi, attacked the contract, which was energetically defended by Antonio Grimani. The contract was accepted, but although 114 members voted in favor, a rather considerable number—41—voted against. Moreover, a majority for the proposal was attained only by a concession. The government would have ten more days before the agreement with Schiapi became final.

Briefly, there was wide agreement about the desirability of accepting a loan from Chigi, and it was admitted that sale of a great amount of alum to the Venetian government formed part of this complicated bargain. But there was resistance against re-selling the alum immediately to one of Chigi's employees: partly, probably, because of the financial loss involved, but partly also because of the immorality of this circumvention of the laws against usury. Thus, after this meeting, a last desperate attempt was made to discover whether there was any Venetian who might want to buy the alum. But nobody dared to take the risk. Another meeting of the Pregadi was called, and the Collegio, evidently impatient with the many delays, declared that the contract had now been discussed four times and that it was necessary to make a final decision.[29] A certain discontent about the bargain, but at the same time a certain helplessness about resisting it, might explain why only a small number of senators attended the meeting. The contract was approved with 83 votes. The various arrangements involved in Chigi's loan could now be signed.

The documents that the Pregadi approved, which were placed in the files of the Senato Secreta where they can still be found, had undergone some changes since the deal with Chigi was first outlined in March and April.[30] The sum of money to be placed at the disposal of the Venetian government was reduced, but also reduced was the difference between the price the Venetian government paid for the alum and the price at which Chigi's employee was to buy it from the government. In its final form, the contract comprised a number of different arrangements. First there was a two-part arrangement with Chigi. The Venetian government agreed to buy from Chigi 7000 cantari of alum at a price of 18 ducats per cantaro.[31] Details about transportation, storage, and taxes—from some of which Chigi was excepted— and about the manner of handing over the alum were included in this part of the document. The second part of the contract was concerned with a loan of 20,000 ducats granted by Chigi to the Venetian government. Alum and loan together amounted to 146,000 ducats. There followed a payment schedule. Venice was to receive Chigi's loan of 20,000 ducats twenty days after the conclusion of the contract, and thirty months later, in 1513, Venice would have to make a payment of 24,333⅓ ducats; and payments in equal size should be made in all the coming years until, after eight years (that means in six payments) the whole amount would have been repaid.

For Venice the advantages seemed clear. Loan and payments for the alum were considered as one debt owed by Venice to Chigi, and the repayment of this debt of 146,000 ducats would have to begin only after two and a half years. On the other hand, Chigi made sure that he would not lose. Fifty Venetian nobles had to pledge with an appropriate part of their capital the repayment of the loan and, at the time of signing of the contract, Chigi would receive jewelry from the treasury of San Marco at the value of 30,000 ducats, which would be restored to Venice when the two last payments of the debt were made.

A simultaneous arrangement addressed the question of the resale of the alum to Alessandro Schiapi. The government agreed to sell him the 7000 cantari of alum for 17 ducats a cantaro; this amounts to 119,000 ducats. Schiapi was to pay 20,000 ducats within two months, the rest to be paid in sums of 16,500 ducats whenever Venice had to make its payments to Chigi: that meant that Schiapi would have to pay for the alum he bought from the Venetian government in six installments. The results was that in order to repay its debt to Chigi, Venice would have to pay, from 1513 on, not 24,333⅓ ducats annually but only 7833½ ducats. On the other hand, Schiapi got the right to sell his alum in Venice for 20 ducats a cantaro, and the government guaranteed that in the next ten years no other alum could be sold in Venice. If Schiapi did not succeed in selling these 7000 cantari within ten years, his monopoly could be prolonged for another three years. Moreover, Schiapi was to receive from the Venetian government rent-free warehouses to store the alum. All these arrangements were secured by elaborate penalties in the case of default.

Altogether this seemed a nicely balanced arrangement: it served the government's current need for cash because Venice was to receive, 20,000 ducats in twenty days after the conclusion of the contract, and another 20,000 ducats two months later. It served Chigi's interests because it secured him a monopoly on the alum trade in Venice. This was important because, as mentioned, Venice was the chief marketplace for alum from sources other than the papal Tolfa mines and where the German merchants preferred to buy. But in the concern of one partner for the present and of the other for the future, there also lay a danger of conflict: What would happen when the immediate threat passed, or when the future looked different from the view in spring of 1511?

A few days after the Pregadi had ended their deliberations on the Chigi arrangements, Sanudo reported a rumor that Chigi was hesitating.[32] There was truth in this rumor—it took almost three months more, until the middle of August, before the contracts were finally signed, and then in much-changed form.

Priuli notes in his diary that Chigi seemed to have regrets

about the contract because "he had now become doubtful of the stability of Venetian affairs, since things were going badly for Venice and its existence was endangered by powerful enemies."[33] Priuli is certainly correct: if at the beginning the negotiations had been interrupted by an earthquake, now another event intervened. This time it was not a natural catastrophe but a sudden catastrophical change in the political and military situation.

S INCE APRIL, the provveditori in the Venetian army camps had been reporting on French preparations for an offensive against the papal and Venetian armies, and as the negotiations with Chigi were reaching a conclusion, the French troops were on the move. Julius II, after a vain attempt to launch a counteroffensive, saw himself in danger of becoming a prisoner if he remained in Bologna. The Venetian government asked its ambassador to dissuade the Pope from leaving because it feared that "the consequence would be rioting and overthrow of the papal regime in Bologna."[34] But their advice was of no avail. Julius II left Bologna on May 21, and two days later the French were in the city, and the Bentivogli, whom five years earlier Julius II had driven out as tyrants and usurpers of Church land, were again established as rulers, to wild popular acclaim and rioting.[35] One irreparable loss was Michelangelo's statue of the Pope over the entrance of the Cathedral of San Petronio; it was severely damaged and later completely destroyed.

But excesses and confusion were still greater on the papal side. The Pope's army dissolved in flight. The governor of Bologna, a cardinal and papal favorite, and the commander of the papal troops, the Duke of Urbino, the Pope's nephew, charged each other with cowardice and responsibility for the defeat. When they met in Ravenna, the irascible young duke killed the cardinal with thrusts of his dagger. Francesco Guicciardini, the great contemporary historian, gave the cardinal an unforgettable, if almost untranslatable, epitaph: "Degno, forse, per tanta degnita di non essere violato, ma degnissimo, per i suoi vizi enormi e injusti, di qualunque acerbissimo suplizio" (Because of his high rank, he might not have deserved to be assaulted, but because of his detestable and inexcusable vices, he did deserve this cruel death). Not only military incompetence but also moral corruption seemed to condemn the papal side to defeat and destruction.

In slow stages Julius II returned to Rome through Rimini and Ancona, where he found notices on the church doors announcing the council that the French king had convoked to put the Pope on trial. Julius arrived in Rome five weeks later, on June 27. By then there were doubts that the Pope could continue his attempt to drive the French out of Italy. He started negotiations with Louis XII, and there was much speculation about his purpose. Did the Pope want to gain time—if so, he achieved this aim because the French king ordered his troops not to advance further—or was he really seeking peace because he considered further military efforts futile?

The Venetians found themselves again in a critical situation. They expected another siege of Padua, and so laid waste the surrounding countryside to deprive their enemies of food and billets. They also feared a threat from the sea since they had heard that Ferdinand of Aragon was fitting out a large fleet that might sail up the Adriatic to Venice. Their own ships were engaged in operations against Ferrara, and the gulf was open. Only very gradually did it become clear that the worst would not happen: the French stopped further military operations and settled down in the countryside, and Ferdinand indicated clearly that he had no intention of attacking Venice.[36]

After a few weeks of despair, the mood in Venice improved. But the Venetians continued to feel extremely insecure. Priuli describes the atmosphere by stating that "good news, even if of little importance, makes them adopt an arrogant attitude, and at the slightest bad news they are inclined to give in and strike the sails."[37] The main worry remained the attitude of the Pope. In Venetian opinion he had three possibilities: he could try to construct a great alliance against France; he might direct all his efforts to bring about an alliance between Maximilian and Venice, which would be attained at Venetian expense and involve great financial and territorial sacrifices; or, if nothing else worked, the Pope might throw himself into the arms of the French king because he might prefer "by good or evil means, not to be deposed but to die as pope."[38] This last possibility was the worst for Venice; it would leave the republic in a hopelessly isolated position.

But if the Venetians were uncertain about the Pope, Chigi was in an even more tenuous position. With Julius moving throughout June slowly down the Adriatic Coast and then over the mountains to Rome, Chigi was cut off from his usual contacts at the Curia and could not know what the Pope planned after the fall of Bologna. Chigi's fortune had been created in Rome at the Curia and continued to depend on it. If the Pope was to turn against Venice, this was not the time to make a big investment. There would be little chance to get his loan repaid or for Venice to become an important market for his alum.

Even in the grimmest days, Julius II never ceased to give signals that he was not willing to give in to the French king. He excommunicated Bologna with "the harshest and cruelest justification that was ever issued by any pope," condemning the people of Bologna and those who supported them into the fourth generation. "They certainly had not sinned or failed toward the pope and did not deserve to be excommunicated," Priuli wrote.[39] Then Julius—in order to counter the council convoked by the French king—declared his intention to hold in Rome in the Lateran a council that was to assemble on September 1, 1512. Such a council in Rome would be merely a device in the hands of the Pope, since "in an authentic council every recent pope from Innocent VIII and Alexander VI to the present pope would have been condemned and dethroned."[40] Even if in the eyes of the contemporaries Julius' desperate measures made him look morally reprehensible, they also demonstrated his indomitable energy. Nevertheless, the question remained whether these measures were primarily tactical, in order to increase the Pope's bargaining strength in negotiations with France, or whether they reflected his will to carry out the slogan "fuori i barbari."

During July this issue became clarified. A certainty about the intentions of Julius II emerged from various developments. The Pope had kept the Venetian ambassador informed about the negotiations with Ferdinand of Aragon and Henry VIII of England to form a league against France, and had also told him that, although Venice was not involved as a chief participant, he wanted Venice to be a member of the league if the negotiations had positive results. In the middle of July reports from Rome announced that, although some financial questions still had to be solved, agreement about the articles of the league had been reached.[41] Further confirmation of Julius' intentions was provided. On July 21 Matthias Schinner, the Swiss cardinal who had enough influence in his country to control the services of the Swiss Landsknechte, arrived in Venice; the purpose of his visit was to obtain 20,000 ducats which the pope had deposited with Chigi and the Venetian bankers for hiring the Landsknechte. Schinner at first had no contact with the Venetian government; but after he had received letters from Rome, he was officially received and treated as a guest of the government; then he sailed on a Venetian galley to meet Julius.[42] Clearly, all this indicated that the Pope was deeply engaged in planning a new campaign against France.

Venice was in a doubtful position at the end of July 1511. The threat of having to conduct alone an almost hopeless struggle against the combined forces of France and Germany had passed. Venice could count on becoming a member of a coalition that was possibly stronger than France and Germany. Venice found itself in a more favorable diplomatic position than it had enjoyed for many years. Nevertheless, at the moment, the situation looked bad. After the pause in military operations that had followed the fall of Bologna, the French, under La Palissa, again moved forward. Without any serious fighting, the Venetian troops began a retreat that became a headlong flight. The Venetian armies disintegrated. Of the terra firma only Padua and Treviso, to which the remnants of the army had retired, remained in Venetian hands. As after Agnadello two years earlier, the Venetian nobles themselves set out to defend these cities, but this emergency measure did not supersede the need for money to reorganize the army—to pay the troops who were still left and to hire new ones.[43] "The Venetian senators are in great desperation and almost worried to death to find *one* ducat," Priuli wrote.[44] He also stated that as a banker he knew what he was talking about: "There is almost no business any more; no trade can develop because the roads are interrupted and often entirely blockaded. Taxes are not paid. The poor cannot pay them and the rich are exhausted, and everyone complains endlessly. Alone the customs produce some income . . . but that is not enough for expenses required by the war."[45] The situation existing at the beginning of the year had returned, and it was even worse than before.

Under these circumstances, as might be expected, interest in the agreement with Chigi revived. Perhaps Chigi did not want to leave Venice before his Venetian business was completed, but it is also likely that, with communications on land interrupted by the French advances, with an uncertain political situation, and with the Pope—on whom everything depended—on the road, he would have been no less cut off from events in Rome than in Venice. Moreover, life in Venice had not entirely lost its splendor and sweetness. In his description of the Venetian financial crisis, Priuli inserted the sentence that, despite the general impoverished state of things, there were still some very rich people in Venice who succeeded in hiding their wealth from the grasp of the rulers.[46] Priuli complained bitterly that unlike their forebears, who had devoted themselves to business and politics, today's youth, even in these dark days, indulged in expensive clothes and precious jewels, rich foods, and gambling. The women too—and this would have been of interest to Chigi, who was a great womanizer—continued to dress luxuriously, according to the latest foreign fashion. Even the needs of the war were turned to purposes of pleasure.

In order to cheer up the people, a tournament was arranged in Mestre,[47] with a horse worth forty ducats as first prize. More than four hundred Venetian nobles, among them many members of the Pregadi, sailed to Mestre to see the spectacle. The competitors were eight Venetian nobles dressed in splendid armor above silken doublets. It is somewhat surprising to find among these eight a well-known name, that of Gasparo Contarini, who later as a cardinal played a crucial role in the struggle of Rome against the Reformation. No matter how bad the political situation was, amusements and entertainments could be found.

Nor was the work of artists interrupted.[48] The Venetian government continued to pay the salary of the painters engaged in decorating the hall of the Great Council and the leaders of the Venetian school of painting, Bellini and Carpaccio, continued to work there. Giorgione, the head of the younger school of painters, had died a few months before Chigi came to Venice, but one of Giorgione's friends and pupils, Titian, was then carrying out his first important commission, the frescoes in the Scuola di San Antonio di Padua.[49] Giorgione's closest collaborator, Sebastiano Luciani (del Piombo) was working in Venice and was then completing Giorgione's last great work, *The Three Philosophers*, for Taddeo Contarini, a Venetian merchant involved in war finances and in business contacts with Chigi.[50]

But during June and July Chigi's existence in Venice was not only marked by enforced leisure. Raphael Besalù, with whom Chigi stayed in Venice at the Palazzo Nani, was his agent, and Besalù's name appears in a number of important business dealings for the import of grain and sale of saltpeter.[51] Undoubtedly Chigi, although his name does not occur in these contracts, participated.

Chigi, though, had one further important concern during these months, and that was the affair which had been the osten-

sible reason for his coming to Venice: the recovery of the money
he claimed was owed him by Alessandro di Franza. When Chigi
arrived in Venice, it was rumored that he wanted to lay his
hands on the treasure of Cesare Borgia with which Franza had
escaped. Probably this rumor arose because Franza and Chigi at
the time of the apex of Cesare's career had helped to finance his
military campaigns. But developments during Chigi's visit in
Venice made it clear that Chigi believed Franza owed him money
for a certain amount of alum sold in Venice for which Chigi had
received no payment. Slowly Chigi's legal efforts bore fruit, and
his suit against Franza came up for decision.[52]

When Chigi arrived in Venice, Franza, who had declared
bankruptcy, left and sailed to Cattaro on the Dalmatian coast.
At the request of Chigi, who was supported by the papal nuncio,
the Venetian government took measures to clear up the affair: it
placed a person who was believed to be Franza's confidant, Fab-
ricio Romano, under arrest and asked the Venetian governor of
Cattaro, Marco Arimondo, to send Franza back to Venice.
Franza fled from Cattaro into the country, which was under
Turkish rule; to get him back into Cattaro, Arimondo gave him
a safe conduct and guaranteed the Turkish governor that the safe
conduct would be strictly observed. On May 20 Franza arrived
in Venice under guard and was immediately put in prison. Having promised safe conduct, did the Venetian government have
the right to incarcerate Franza? The legal complications were so
great that only after long delays, on July 8, did the case come
before the Quarantia.

Evidently there was great pressure to decide against Franza.
The Doge himself and his counselors were present; the papal
nuncio and Chigi attended, their chairs placed next to the Doge's,
and they were allowed to present their own case, although their
right to do so was doubtful. Both parties were represented by
lawyers of great repute. Despite the pressure put on the Quarantia by the government, the outcome was in favor of Franza. Nine
members of the Quarantia voted against him, seven abstained,

and twenty-five voted to release him. After he was freed, the government intervened forcefully. The head of the Council of Ten, supported by the Collegio, required the Quarantia to give the case another hearing, and on July 15, after the case had been discussed in several sessions, the Quarantia, in the presence of the Doge, reversed itself. With a small majority they decided to keep Franza in prison. In the last days of July, a special emissary of the Pope, Antonio della Sassetta, arrived from Rome and presented to the Collegio the demand that Franza be sent to Rome because the sums he had embezzled derived from the sale of alum and therefore had belonged to the papal treasury; thus the case ought to be decided before an ecclesiastical court. The Venetian government declared that it would take this request under consideration. Franza remained in Venetian prisons for two more years, until July 1513, when he was released because nothing could be found against him.[53]

IT SEEMS more than likely that Chigi used the Franza affair as a mild kind of blackmail against the Venetian government. The great interest that the Doge and the Collegio manifested in the outcome of the dispute suggests that Chigi had hinted that his willingness to resume loan negotiations would be increased if the suit resulted in his favor. He increased the pressure by bringing in help from the Curia. Unquestionably Chigi would have been informed about the developments of the diplomatic situation by his Venetian acquaintances, but he might have found still more decisive the direct information that the Roman emissary had provided. Clearly, by the beginning of August it had become evident to him that the Pope and Venice would remain on the same side in the war. In this respect there was no further obstacle to a conclusion of the loan.

And so the final act took place. There was one further important change in the contract. That part of the agreement which provided for resale of the alum to Alessandro Schiapi was dropped. It was replaced by an understanding that the Venetians ought to decide after six months whether they wanted to repay the loan or carry out the contract in the form originally stipulated, that is, to buy 7000 cantari of alum from Chigi. In this case Chigi obligated himself to find a person to whom they could resell the alum immediately. Before the six months had passed, meaning that as long as the Venetians had not decided to buy the alum from Chigi, Chigi was guaranteed that only his alum, no other alum, would be permitted to appear on the Venetian market and that he could sell it in Venice at the high price of 20 ducats a cantaro.[54]

In short, the Venetian government received an interest-free loan of 20,000 ducats. Chigi received as security for the loan jewels from the treasury of San Marco and pledges from fifty prominent Venetian citizens to the amount of 1000 ducats each. Moreover, he had a promise from the Venetian government to protect his alum monopoly and not to interfere in the sale price if it did not go beyond 20 ducats a cantaro.

Priuli, speaking of this agreement, was bitter about Chigi: "With little love and charity, perhaps even desiring Venice's fall, in knowledge of Venice's urgent needs and aware that the Venetian Republic was in great difficulties and in danger of complete collapse, he tightened the rope around our neck more and more to his own utility and profit."[55] Clearly it was to Chigi's advantage to have this alum monopoly. But it must also be said that, although the jewels and the pledges covered the loan more than adequately, the loan was interest-free and, despite the prohibition of usury, loans were almost never given without some compensation. Moreover, the Venetians themselves may have been quite glad to delay the decision about the alum sale. The Holy League that was in the process of formation created an entirely new situation. It was true that the existing threat against Padua and Treviso and the dissolution of Venetian armed strength in the terra firma required immediate expenditures of great sums of cash. But it was more difficult to foresee what expenses would be demanded from Venice when the League began to function. Nor did it seem entirely impossible that the intervention of the Swiss and of Spain might soon end the war. Finally, as we have seen, Antonio Tron had just presented the ruling group with a strong challenge—the acceptance of an undeniably usurious contract could only increase murmuring and discontent.

As to the manner in which the contract was viewed by many Venetian nobles, Girolamo Priuli probably can serve as a model. He was convinced of the necessity of getting this loan. Through his father, a recent controller, he was intimately informed about the financial difficulties of the government and the desperate attempts that had been made to obtain cash. During these months Venice's financial difficulties form a main theme of his diary. Priuli considered the freedom and independence of the Venetian Republic inextricably tied to maintaining control over Padua and Treviso; organization of an army that could defend these two cities was of paramount importance. Chigi's 20,000 ducats were necessary, no matter what the conditions. "Jus violandum est regnandi causa."[56] Nevertheless, the admission that it was necessary to conclude the agreement did not mean that in his eyes the contract was anything but "shameful and harmful."[57]

The distaste for concluding the agreement came out into the open once again at the end of these long-drawn-out negotiations. On August 1, in a general discussion of the contract in its most recent form, two members of the Tron family tried in vain to stop the consent of the Senate; again Antonio Grimani was the main defender of the contract.[58] Then on August 6 the agreement was taken up for the last time. Chigi had put together a list of fifty senators whom he wanted as guarantors with their pledges of 1000 ducats each.[59] When the Senate met and the fifty were called upon to sign the document, twelve were absent and, when found, refused to sign. Now the Doge intervened for one more time, emphasizing the urgent need for the loan and asking other senators to undertake the obligation. More than the required number of senators rose and declared themselves willing to take

on this commitment. Even now Antonio Tron remained adamant in refusing to make a pledge. But among those who signed,
we find a great many of those families who had celebrated
Chigi's arrival in Venice in February: Grimani, Bembo, Pisani,
Cappelli, Corner, Trevisan, Emo, Molino—advocates of the
political connection with the Pope.[60]

Chigi now gave power to his agent, Raphael Besalù, to complete the technical details of the deal.[61] On the day following the
final Senate meeting, Chigi together with his principal support-
ers during the extended negotiations—Antonio Grimani, Andrea
Venier, Angelo Trevisan, Pietro Balbi—was seen entering the
sacristy of San Marco to inspect the jewels he would receive as
security.[62] Ten days later Chigi left by ship for Rome.[63] He took
with him on board two persons. One was the painter, Sebastiano
Luciani, who soon after his arrival in Rome began to work for
Chigi in the Villa Farnesina. The other was his Venetian mistress,
Francesca Ordeaschi, whom some years later he made his wife.

PALMA GIOVANE, ALLEGORY OF VENICE
AND THE LEAGUE OF CAMBRAI.
Alinari / Editorial Photocolor Archives

PERUZZI, PAINTING FROM THE CEILING OF THE VILLA FARNESINA.
Alinari

VENETIE
MD

BARBARI, VENICE, 1500.
Alinari / Editorial Photocolor Archives

Upper left: Antonio Grimani as Procurator of San Marco.
Victoria and Albert Museum
Upper right: Andrea Gritti as Procurator of San Marco.
National Gallery of Art, Samuel H. Kress Foundation
Center: Julius II. *National Gallery of Art,*
Samuel H. Kress Foundation
Below (obverse and reverse of medal): Agostino Chigi.
British Museum

Chigi in Rome:
The Pope's Favorite

P RIULI SUGGESTS in his diary that Chigi vacillated from May to August about the loan to the Venetian government because he felt uncertain about events on the rapidly changing political scene and had doubts about Venice's chances of survival. Evidently Priuli believed that political considerations played a role in Chigi's negotiations. But to what extent did politics enter into Chigi's plans? Was he a businessman who looked upon political developments primarily from the point of view of the risks he ran in making an investment, or did he use the power his wealth gave him for political purposes? Chigi lived in Rome; the sources of his wealth were in the papal states. The question of the importance that political considerations had in his business transactions turns on Chigi's relations to papal policy and particularly to Julius II.

Neither historical narratives nor biographical treatments provide much information on Chigi's connections with papal policy. Sixteenth-century historians are remarkably unsatisfactory about the role of economic and financial considerations in political decisions. Certainly it is recognized that expenses for military enterprises were a heavy burden and that rulers were inclined to be prodigal; however, figures are usually exaggerated. Moreover, there is a definite reluctance to acknowledge that actions in foreign policy might have economic motivations or be tied to financial interests. This attitude is a legacy of the ancient world: humanist historians follow the pattern laid out in the writings of classical historians, and they regard foreign policy as identical with war and wars as consisting of movements of armies and

battles. Politics on one side, finances and economics on the other
—this was a strict division in the minds of narrative historians.

The first biography of Chigi was composed in the seventeenth
century by his great-nephew, Fabio Chigi, who became Pope
Alexander VII.[1] Although later writers have added valuable
material, they accepted the outline of Agostino's life that Fabio
had given. Fabio described Agostino as the richest man of his
time, who got his wealth because he directed and controlled all
the important economic resources of the papacy. Agostino was
greatly honored by princes and was a patron of artists and writers. All this does not get us very far. If we want to establish the
role that politics played in the life and actions of this papal
banker, we must unravel his entire life: we must find out how he
came to his wealth, whether this quest involved him in the politics of Rome, and what his relations to the leading men of the
Curia were. So far we have seen Chigi only as he was seen by his
Venetian hosts. Now we must try to understand his actions by
studying the experiences that determined his thinking.

WHENEVER Agostino Chigi's name appears in official documents or business contracts, he is called "mercator Senensis Romanam Curiam sequens." He is, of course, only one of the
Sienese bankers in Rome to whom this characterization is applied, and similar formulas are used to designate bankers from
other Italian cities; for instance, Florentines are "mercatores
Fiorentini Romanam Curiam sequentes."[2] Bankers were thus
titled when they were engaged in business with the financial administration of the Roman Curia over many years. The financial
transactions that took place at the Curia were of a most varied
character and were conducted by several agencies with different
bankers and businessmen, among whom the "mercatores Romanam curiam sequentes" formed a special group.[3]

The Dataria, an office managed by clerics, had important
functions: it handled the sale of all those curial offices with secu-

lar tasks administered by laymen. The Dataria also received the payments for privileges, dispensations, and indulgences. Since many of these indulgences were offered to the faithful living outside Italy, the money they brought in had to be transferred to Rome and required the services of bankers. Such transfer operations were needed also for the great variety of payments from different parts of Europe due to the Pope as head of the ecclesiastical organization: annates, servitia, tithes. These transactions were frequently undertaken by non-Italians; the sale of indulgences, for instance, made the Fugger a financial power in Rome within the first twenty years of the sixteenth century.[4]

The Italian bankers and merchants residing in Rome were involved in some of such transfer operations, but their main activities lay elsewhere. They were moneylenders and were concerned with the raising of taxes in the territories under direct control of the Pope: the papal states.[5] These two activities—the advancing of loans and the managing, or farming, of tax revenues—were clearly connected. In certain respects tax farming itself was a form of moneylending: at the beginning of each of the years of his contract, the tax farmer paid a sum to the papal treasurer for which he was compensated from the tax revenue only at a later time, although he expected that the tax revenue he received in the course of the year would amount to a sum greater than what he paid out at the beginning of the year. The same bankers were also expected to grant loans to the Pope in case of need, and it is clear that this kind of service was a precondition for favorable treatment in getting a valuable tax-farming contract from the Curia.[6]

The peculiar nature and structure of the papal state made tax farming a very profitable business. The papal state was, as Jacob Burckhardt said, "a thorough anomaly among the powers of Italy."[7] The popes were the overlords of powerful rulers like the kings of Naples or the dukes of Ferrara and Urbino. They had as vassals troublesome clans like the Colonna and Orsini, who owned vast estates, and they were suzerains of nobles who possessed only small stretches of land around their castles. The popes ruled over large towns like Bologna and Perugia, in which the inhabitants were struggling against the tyranny of families like the Bentivogli and Baglioni, and they had in their dominion free communes like Ancona.

Although this political structure was very fragile and contin-ued to exist only because, as Burckhardt said, "here the spiritual power could constantly conceal or supply the defects of the temporal," the diversity of this chequered formation was not reflected in the organization of the financial administration—that was complex, but it worked throughout the papal states along similar, almost identical, lines. Of course, the great, almost independent vassals of the Pope—Naples, Ferrara, Urbino—had their own financial administration, and they fulfilled their obligation to their overlord by one annual payment on the day of the feast of St. Peter and Paul: the Duke of Ferrara paid 4000 ducats, the Duke of Urbino 1400 ducats, and the king of Naples gave the Pope a white horse.[8] Fixed annual tributes were also paid by some of the owners of landed estates. The payments of some of the holders of small estates were quite insignificant; a few of the free communes raised their own taxes and paid a fixed amount to the apostolic chamber.

Nevertheless, with the exception of Ferrara and Urbino, the Curia had established in its territories its own system for raising taxes. The revenues of the Curia were of two kinds. One was called subsidy (sussidio), a name under which the customary direct and indirect taxes—a hearth tax and customs and duties on exports and imports—were subsumed. The other source of revenue came from the papal salt monopoly, which was administered independently from the subsidy. For the purposes of collecting taxes, the papal states were divided into a number of administrative units: on one hand, provinces—the Romagna, the Campagna, the Marches, and the Patrimony of St. Peter—on the other hand, large towns—Bologna, Perugia, and of course Rome. In each of these districts two officials were entrusted with the raising of revenues; one, the "treasurer," was responsible for the subsidy, the other was responsible for collecting revenues from the salt monopoly. Because of its size and economic importance, Rome had a distinct organization for its financial administration.[9] Duties were to be paid on imports coming by land,[10] on imports coming on the Tiber or by sea,[11] on imports of meat and foodstuffs;[12] the collection of each of these duties was in the hands of a special officer. Also, the tax on wine, which had the attractive name of university tax because part of its revenue paid the salaries of university professors,[13] had its special collector, as had the tax to be paid for the right of grazing.[14] The revenues raised by the various collectors or tax farmers went to the chief collector of revenues,[15] who was the highest lay official in the financial administration of the Curia: he received instructions from the clerics in the apostolic chamber who were directed by the chamberlain, who was always a cardinal.

Tax farming at the Curia could be profitable, but it was also risky. If well managed, the revenues could far surpass the amount that the tax farmer had to pay annually to the Curia, and the position contained opportunities for useful contacts and patronage. But it was necessary to make quick full use of the opportunities. The leases were limited in time, usually three years, and there could be developments—whether by human action, such as war, or by divine intervention, such as bad harvests—which reduced the income during the term of the lease. Renewals of the contract with the tax-farming banker might be made dependent on the granting of additional loans. And the sudden death of a pope or an influential cardinal might end all chances for getting repayment of the loans. Only firms with strong resources— mostly several firms acting in association—could enter this field of financial activity.

Because of the efforts and risks involved, the bankers at the Curia were not equally interested in all the taxes that were farmed out. Some of them were not available to them—for instance, the Bentivogli took care that the collecting of taxes in Bologna went to Bolognese citizens.[16] The farming of some other taxes was hardly profitable because the revenue that could be drawn from them was either very small or, as in the case of the taxes to be raised by the treasurer of Benivent, was almost entirely absorbed by the salaries for the governor, the castellan, and other local officials. Among the collectors of such revenues, the designation "mercatores Romanam Curiam sequentes" rarely appears. But other taxes could be sources of great income, and they aroused the cupidity of merchants and bankers: of all taxes, the Roman salt tax was estimated to produce the highest revenue.[17] Other rich sources were the taxes collected by the treasurer of the Marches[18] and the salt tax of this province.[19] Almost equally valuable were the revenues from the taxes and customs in the district of Rome: the duties on imports coming by ship,[20] those on imports coming by land,[21] the duties for the right of grazing in Rome and the patrimony of St. Peter.[22] The income from the food and meat tax was also high, but from it had to be paid the salaries of the officials of the city of Rome and of the Castle of Sant' Angelo.[23]

The amounts the tax-farming banker had to make annually to the Curia went to the chief collector of taxes. Clearly the office of the chief collector was the most desirable position that a "mercator Romanam Curiam sequens" could obtain. He might have considerable cash at his disposal when the time came for him to make disbursements, or, as it happened more often, he might have to advance money if expenses had to be met before the revenues had arrived. Every chief collector became deeply involved in moneylending, not only in order to bridge temporary gaps between expenses and income but also to give large loans to the Pope for his personal needs or for political and military purposes.[24] Such loans could be very profitable, but the chief collector was not always sure that he would have the needed means at his disposal at a given moment. Therefore, he usually acted in close cooperation with other banking firms, preferably conducted by merchants from his own town. These associations would bolster his financial resources if an occasion arose that demanded an outlay greater than his own liquid capital. But the chief collector, by means of his influence and by means of the revenues at his disposal, could secure privileges and advantages for his associates and help them to succeed in bids for profitable taxes. A chief collector of revenue was a man of great power and influence in papal Rome.[25]

In the early 1490s, when Agostino Chigi began to play a role in Roman financial life, the chief collector was Antonio Spannocchi from the Sienese firm called Heirs of Ambrogio de Spannocchi and Associates.[26] In emphasizing that the firm traced its origin back to Ambrogio de Spannocchi, the members of the Spannocchi firm were indicating that their business had a long tradition of financial activity at the Roman Curia. Ambrogio had been chief collector from 1455 to 1464. He had followed Cosimo de' Medici, who was appointed by Pope Nicholas V, intimate of Florentine humanists. Ambrogio de Spannocchi was selected as chief collector by the first Borgia pope, Calixtus III, under whom Cardinal Aeneas Silvius Piccolomini from Siena had been a dominating influence in the Curia. When Aeneas Silvius Piccolomini became Pope Pius II, Ambrogio remained chief collector until the end of Pius' reign in 1464. It was natural that when Alexander VI, another Borgia, became pope in 1492, the position of chief collector was again given to the Spannocchi firm, which was now directed by three sons of Ambrogio: Antonio, Alessandro, and Giuliano. Among them, Antonio was the outstanding figure.

After some years the Spannocchi managed to remove many of the previous tax farmers and were able to lay their hands on most of the profitable sources of revenue in the administration of the papal states.[27] The number of lucrative offices they had accumulated by the year 1500 was remarkable.[28] At Christmas of 1500, they took over the administration of the Roman salt tax, which was given to them for seven years; they held the salt tax of the Romagna and of Perugia, both also for seven years; for three years, beginning in 1499, they were treasurers of the Marches and of the salt tax of that province, and had farmed the Roman wine tax. As I have mentioned, the salt tax in Rome and the taxes in the Marches brought the highest revenues of all the papal taxes. Administration of the two next valuable taxes—those on import to Rome by ship or by land—were in the hands of a Sienese banking firm, a close associate of the Spannocchi, the firm of Stefan de Ghinucci. When Ambrogio de Spannocchi became chief collector in 1455, the Ghinucci were his business partners, and the two firms of the Spannocchi and Ghinucci continued to work together. Furthermore, the valuable Roman tax on food and meat was in the hands of a relative of the Spannocchi: the treasurer of the Patrimony of St. Peter, Alessandro di Franza whom we have met already. Finally, an employee in the Spannocchi bank, Alessandro de Lenis, was farmer of the taxes to be paid at the Gates of Rome.

AGOSTINO CHIGI began his career in the financial world of Rome as a member of the group around the Spannocchi. Agostino's father, Mariano, was a banker in Siena, and in Siena the Chigi were no less important than the Spannocchi or Ghinucci. But the Chigi had no bank in Rome and Agostino and one of his brothers, who died soon after,[29] were sent to Rome to give the Chigis representation at the Curia. On March 31, 1487, either at the time that Chigi went to Rome or shortly thereafter, Mariano made a contract with Stefan de Ghinucci and his associates according to which his son Agostino would become partner in the Ghinucci firm ("Iniat Societatem"); for this purpose, Mariano invested 2000 ducats in the Ghinucci firm.[30] In case of dissolution of the firm, one half of the Chigi share would go to Agostino, the other to Mariano and the rest of his heirs.

Agostino had received his first business training in Siena and Viterbo in the bank of one of his future associates, Francesco

Tommasi, and the training seems to have continued during his first years in Rome.[31] Agostino quickly acquired self-confidence because he told his father that money Mariano intended to invest in the Ghinucci bank would bring greater profits if entrusted to him. By the mid-1490s Chigi's apprenticeship was over. He came out as his own man in the Roman business world. In June 1494, he farmed the tax on the grazing rights in the Patrimony, at first for three years; the contract was then prolonged several times until 1505.[32] In the same summer, Chigi bought grain for the papal household because Alexander VI considered the grain grown in the region of Siena as of particularly good quality.[33] In the next year, 1495, Agostino acquired for 11,000 ducats a three-year lease on the tax on overland imports to Rome.[34] Agostino's reputation as a banker of means and ability was now established. He was much sought after; he gave a loan of 4000 ducats to Piero de' Medici, for which he received tapestries, jewels, and furniture—originally as security although it was probably clear to everyone that Piero would not be able to pay this debt and the pledged valuables would come into Chigi's full possession.[35] This was the beginning of Chigi's connection with the Medici, which continued to the time when Cardinal Giovanni Medici, to whom Chigi had given several loans, became Pope Leo X.

Agostino did business with other Italian ruling families. He transferred money for the Duke of Urbino, Guidobaldo da Montefeltre.[36] His most important contact at this time, however, was with Cesare Borgia. Chigi stayed with Cesare in November and December 1499, when Cesare conducted his campaign for the conquest of the towns of the Romagna, and he assisted Cesare in getting a loan from the Spannocchi for this military enterprise.[37] Agostino's procedure in this situation shows that, although he had attained a recognized position as a financier, he still drew a good part of his credit from being a member of the powerful group of Sienese bankers. An indication of this is the fact that in several of his enterprises, particularly in his business with the apostolic chamber, he and Alessandro di Franza appear as associates.[38] It is not surprising that a man as conscious of his ability and as energetic as Chigi would not be satisfied with a position as a member of a team. Chigi looked around for an opportunity that would give him a more independent field of action, and he became interested in the possibility of administering the exploitation of the alum mines at Tolfa, north of Rome; the lease was in the hands of the "heirs of Paolo Rucellai," a Florentine bank at the Roman Curia, but it was to expire in May 1501. Agostino was aware that in his application for this lease he needed the support of the Spannocchi. By giving them a share in the profits of the Tolfa mines and paying Pope Alexander VI an advance of 7000 ducats on the grazing tax and an advance of 20,000 ducats on the Tolfa revenue, he could acquire the lease to the mines.[39] This was the decisive step in Chigi's career, and the agreement was given a form which shows that Chigi had given much thought to this enterprise.

The "Appaltum Alluminum Sanctae Cruciatae et Camerae Apostolicae," as the contract was called, was for the same length of time as the one with the Rucellai had been, for twelve years. But Chigi's contract differed from previous contracts in that he obligated himself to pay annually a fixed sum of 15,000 ducats; production and sale of the alum were entirely left to him. Previously the apostolic chamber itself engaged in selling alum in certain areas and received a percentage from the profit of the rest of the sales. In comparison to the uncertain revenues from the mines in earlier years, the change made in the contract with Chigi was advantageous for the apostolic chamber but also gave Chigi greater scope for action. He was the only manager, although he was supposed to consult with the Spannocchi and to give them exact accounts. They would receive two fifths of the profits.[40] Agostino would keep the rest.

Until this time Chigi had acted as a partner of the Ghinucci bank or on behalf of "Mariano Chigi and heirs." Having obtained the lease to the Tolfa mines he needed formal recognition as an independent businessman and entrepreneur, and this step was soon taken. In May 1502, one year after the Tolfa contract had come into force, a new company to last for three years, with the possibility of prolongation for an additional five years, was set up with the purpose of conducting business ("per fare trafico et traficare") at the Curia.[41] It was formed by three partners, Mariano Chigi, Agostino Chigi, and Francesco Tommasi, all of Sienese origin. The capital of the company amounted to 8000 ducats of which Mariano and Agostino provided 3250 ducats each, Tommasi 1500. Tommasi was expected to stay in Rome to be in contact with the Curia. Mariano was expected to be in Rome six months of each of the following three years. Agostino, however, would be engaged in the current business only as far as it suited him. Agostino clearly was the leading figure in this company. Whereas the business Mariano and Tommasi might do in Rome had be done within the framework of the company, Agostino was entitled to do business on his own account. Moreover, the business place of the company was to be Agostino's house.

Agostino, "mercator Senensis Romanam Curiam sequens," now had a variety of sources of revenue: he was a tax farmer, he directed the Tolfa mines, and he had a company of his own. Did he chafe at the reins that bound him to the Spannocchi, and did he try to free himself? This seems likely if we take later events into account. But such an assumption is based on hindsight: for the Borgia period, no clear or definite indication exists of such an attitude on Chigi's part.

It was the death of Alexander VI in August 1503 which changed the situation at the Curia and became critical for Chigi's further career. At first the end of the Borgias seemed to leave the situation unaltered, insofar as the financial administration of the Curia was concerned. The Spannocchi and Ghinucci made a contract with the College of Cardinals, according to which they would spend up to 15,000 ducats for the purpose of arranging the funeral of Alexander VI and making the necessary installations for the conclave; they expected to be repaid within a year but kept as security jewels from the papal palace and the revenues they drew as treasurers of the Marches and collectors of the salt tax there. They were also assured that they would be entitled to keep these positions until the debt had been paid off.[42] They may have been particularly anxious to get these pledges because Antonio Spannocchi, the chief collector of revenues, had died a few days before Alexander VI, and they were fearful of losing this important position; they could soon feel reassured. Pius III, the successor of the Borgia pope, was a Piccolomini from Siena. When, after his coronation, he descended from the altar, he turned to Giuliano Spannocchi and appointed him chief collector, reminding him with tears in his eyes that Ambrogio Spannocchi, Giuliano's father, had fulfilled the same function under the pope's uncle, Pius II.[43]

But the second Piccolomini pope died within the first month of his reign and was succeeded by Julius II, a strong ruler, remote, vehemently opposed to the situation that had developed under the Borgias. It has been regarded as a sign of the great impression that Chigi made on those who met him and of his remarkable diplomatic gifts that he was able to be in the good graces of three popes, all of strong character but of very different stamp: Alexander VI, Julius II, Leo X. Because of the influence the Sienese bankers exerted on the financial affairs of the Curia under Alexander VI, the rise of the brilliantly endowed son of a rich Sienese banker at the Borgia Curia should not surprise us. Nor is Chigi's eminence in the times of the Medici pope astounding. Chigi had shown financial favors to the Medici for many years before Giovanni Medici became Pope Leo X. Moreover, Chigi's house was one of Rome's most famous villas. He was a friend and patron of Raphael and other artists whom Leo X himself favored; as promoter of humanist studies and protector of writers, Chigi was a leading figure in fields which, since the fifteenth century, the Medici had cultivated. Leo X had every reason to regard Chigi as an ornament of his court. Nevertheless, he never belonged to Leo's most intimate circle, the Bibbiena, Castiglione, Bembo, Rucellai, and Sadoleto. And it is almost more surprising that

Chigi was not more influential and prominent at the court of the Medici pope than that he was a well-known figure in Leo's Rome.

But the fact that Chigi acquired the favor and even the friendship of Julius II is an astonishing feat. Julius regarded the Borgias with passionate hatred, and he extended these feelings to those who had enjoyed the Borgias' favor. Julius, who moved out of the Borgia apartments in the Vatican because he did not want to be reminded of those Borgias "of cursed memory," returned many of the territories the Borgias had conquered to their former owners—the Sforzas, Gaetanis, Colonnas, and Orsinis.[44] He abolished or changed the financial contracts that under Alexander VI had been concluded "against the interest and to the disadvantage of the apostolic chamber."[45] Following tradition, he appointed Paolo Sauli, a banker from his native Genoa, to be chief collector of revenues, and soon the Sauli, as under Alexander VI the Spannocchi, became farmers of some of the most important taxes of the papal states. They were farmers of the Roman salt tax from 1504 on, and a few years later they leased the taxes on the right of grazing and on overland import to Rome. They became treasurers in Perugia and Umbria. Briefly, the Sauli succeeded the Spannocchi—the influence of the Sienese bankers was replaced by that of the Genoese.[46] But Agostino Chigi was not affected by Julius' campaign against the Borgias and their adherents. He remained farmer of the Tolfa mines, and his contract was expressly confirmed early in 1504.[47]

There is one obvious explanation of the preferential treatment that Chigi received. Giuliano della Rovere's election as Pope Julius II was openly flaunted simony.[48] Although distribution of the many benefices he had accumulated since his early years would have given him quite a number of votes, he undoubtedly needed great amounts of money for further inducements. "One talks not of hundreds but of thousands and ten thousand ducats," reported the Venetian ambassador from Rome. Contemporaries already pointed to Chigi as one of those who provided

Giuliano della Rovere with a large portion of the money by which he bought himself into the papacy. And although, as can be expected in the case of such transactions, no proof is available, it is more than likely that this was done, that Chigi loaned Giuliano great amounts of money. It might also not be unjustified to suggest that, just as the Spannocchi had made as a condition of a loan to the cardinals the maintenance of their positions in the financial administration of the church, Chigi also had insisted that, with Giuliano's election, he would remain farmer of the papal alum mines.

But when the newly elected Pope, after having conceded Chigi a continuation of the contract, took a look at the results of Chigi's management of the Tolfa mines, he might also have been impressed by the work Chigi had done: the revenue that the papal chamber received from the Tolfa mines was more regular and probably higher than it had been under previous farmers. The mining operation was better organized; it concentrated on the most productive veins and employed men who had worked in the alum mines of Asia Minor. Chigi had built up a sales organization in the larger towns of Italy, in Lyons and London, and had contracts with merchants in other parts of Europe.[49] Clearly Chigi was engaged in a serious attempt to make a reality out of the monopoly that, according to the bull Pius II had issued in 1463, soon after the discovery of the mines, the alum of Tolfa ought to have in all the markets of Christian Europe. The interests of pope and banker ran parallel. Chigi wanted to make use of all the possibilities that the riches of the Tolfa mines offered. Julius II, through all the baffling turns of his dramatic policy, constantly pursued one aim—to maintain all the territory and all the rights the papacy possessed and to regain those it had lost. The Pope saw clearly to what extent the monopoly of the Tolfa alum on the European market assisted not only his finances but reinforced his authority in Europe. This monopoly was one of the papal rights that needed to be maintained and strengthened. It was the link that brought pope and banker together in a cooperation that quickly intensified. That they had started out in opposing camps was soon forgotten.

THE HIGHPOINT of Chigi's career was the ten years from 1503 to 1513, when Julius II sat on the papal throne. But although Chigi was the best-known financier at the papal court, he was not all-powerful and not the only banker who counted. It is true that the Spannocchi declined quickly, and Chigi might have had a hand in this.[50] In January 1504, Raphael Besalù, who had been the representative of the Spannocchi in Venice, transferred to the Chigi firm and became their agent.[51] Chigi also terminated the partnership of the Spannocchi in the alum business with the consequences of a long lawsuit.[52] The Ghinucci continued to lease valuable taxes from the apostolic chamber,[53] and Chigi may have given them some assistance. But banking firms that had nothing to do with Chigi began to develop into important factors in the financial administration of the Curia. The bank of the Fugger in Rome, which had been established in 1495 and had been chiefly concerned with transfer of papal revenues from Germany, increased in importance and resources when the popes, first Julius II and then Leo X, discovered the financial usefulness of frequent offerings of indulgences, particularly to the German people.[54]

Most of all, the Sauli, with their roots in the powerful banking community of Genoa, and as chief collectors strongly entrenched in Roman financial life, were rich and influential. Chigi, who as a farmer of the Tolfa mines paid an annual fixed sum to the apostolic chamber, could keep his affairs separate from the financial transactions with which the chief collector was concerned. Whether it was an accidental development or a conscious action, Chigi and Sauli seem to have taken great care not to encroach upon each other's territory. This did not mean that the Chigis no longer had any share in the benefits that bankers could derive from the financial administration of the Curia. For five years, from 1510 on, they were treasurers in the Patrimony, and in 1511 Chigi leased the revenues of the tax on grazing rights.[55] But there was no attempt on the part of the Chigi firm to dominate the administration of the revenues of the papal states.

Chigi's chief aim was to remain in undisturbed possession of his main asset: the exploitation of the Tolfa mines. Of course, he was engaged in many other enterprises for which his revenues from the mines provided him with more than the necessary resources. We find him as a partner in companies trading in silk and cloth; at times, he acted as a grain merchant; he advanced money to condottieri; and he granted loans to the great and powerful: the Pope, members of the Medici family, cardinals.[56] The most spectacular loan was that of 50,000 ducats given in the time of Leo X to Cardinal Riario, in order to free him from the prison into which he had been thrown because he had been involved in a conspiracy against the pope's life.[57] But the basis for Chigi's financial transactions, the capital he needed for the great variety of his business enterprises, came from the Tolfa mines. Their management also demonstrated his financial genius because he was the first to make full use of the opportunities inherent in this enterprise—that is, the monopoly the popes had given to the Tolfa mines in Christian Europe.[58]

Chigi divided Europe into different regions; in each of them he had either an agent who sold alum on Chigi's behalf, or he made a contract with a merchant living abroad who received the right to sell alum in a strictly limited area and was to share the proceeds with Chigi. For instance, he made a contract with Girolamo Boninsegni in Sicily that he would receive 8000 cantari of alum to be sold in Sicily and Spain; Chigi guaranteed that no other alum would be sent to this region within the next two years. Chigi also tried to reduce costs and strengthen his position by eliminating dependence on the use of foreign ships. In 1507, he leased from the government of Siena for fifty years—in compensation for a loan of 8000 ducats—a small town on the coast of southern Tuscany, Porto Ercole, and its castle.[59] Besides the obligation to support Siena in case of war and, if grain had to be imported, to import it only from Sienese territory, there was no other restriction on Chigi's sovereignty over Porto Ercole. He received the revenues from taxes and administered justice there. If Siena wanted to reacquire Porto Ercole after fifty years, they would have to repay the loan Chigi had given them. This lease, which caused Chigi more trouble than he had counted on—in letters he spoke of "this damned Porto Ercole"[60]—fulfilled two purposes. He could store alum in his own magazines and have a harbor for his ships. Chigi could never dispense with the services of foreign, particularly Genoese and Venetian, ships, but from 1509 on Chigi's ships appear on the list of alum carriers.[61]

Chigi's plans for making the alum monopoly fully effective encountered some serious obstacles. Monopolistic possession of an essential raw material by one person or group usually spurs a quest for the discovery of other sources of this raw material, and these searches are often successful. This certainly happened in the case of alum. In Naples at Agnano, in Spain near Cartagena, and in France, alum deposits were discovered. Chigi succeeded in making an agreement that the mines of Agnano, which belonged to the poet Jacopo Sannazaro, would restrict their annual production and sell it only to him. His attempts to get control of the alum discovered near Cartagena were less successful, but little of this alum was exported and it did not represent serious competition on the European market. The French king was not willing to acknowledge the monopoly of the Tolfa mines, and in 1507, he placed high duties on the import of alum. But the French mines were not very productive, so that the duties had soon to be lowered again and French alum too presented no serious competition to Tolfa.[62]

Although for reasons of principle, Chigi opposed the opening of alum mines in other regions of Christian Europe, competition from French and Spanish alum was not of great concern. Alum was essential and needed in great quantities in the cloth and glass industries. Thus, the crucial markets for Chigi were in northern

Europe and Italy: in the north, the Low Countries and England were important; and in Italy, Venice was essential. Venice also needed alum for trade, since it was the point of departure for overland transportation of alum to southern Germany and its cloth-manufacturing Free Cities. In these areas, economic prosperity depended to a great degree on having a regular supply of alum at reasonable prices. So the real threat to the Tolfa monopoly came from the alum mines of Asia Minor, now in the hands of the Turks. In the Low Countries and England, there was a very strong inclination to place material interests above religious scruples. Such an attitude was facilitated by Chigi's ruthless exploitation of his alum monopoly: he kept the amount of alum he offered on these markets low and the price high.

In England, the price that Chigi asked was regarded as so outrageous that a royal ship was ordered to bring Turkish alum to England. This open revolt against the papal monopoly finally ended in a compromise: the English king agreed to prohibit the sale of Turkish alum in England for five years, and he expected Chigi's managers in England to import annually 5000 cantari of alum: no other alum would be allowed on the English market and the duty on the import of the alum would be reduced. Chigi also had to make concessions. The price to be paid for his alum was set low. Moreover, the money he received would have to be invested in English goods, mainly cloth. And the alum would have to be transported on a royal ship or on ships designated by the king. For this service a sum of 1000 "marks" would have to be paid annually. Finally, Chigi and his associates were to ask the Pope to lift the excommunication of those who had brought Turkish alum into England.[63]

At the same time, another conflict took place with the merchants and the government of the Low Countries. The cloth merchants of Bruges and Ghent complained that Chigi was sending insufficient amounts of alum to Flanders and that he had raised the price four or five times over the old price. As a countermeasure, the government ordered the import of Turkish alum, and a Florentine firm, Frescobaldi and Gualterotti, brought Turkish alum over from England into Flanders. Immediately the price of alum went down. When Rome protested this violation of the papal monopoly, the government of the Netherlands reacted sharply: all the alum of the Tolfa mines stored in the Low Countries, at an estimated value of 80,000 ducats, was confiscated. Here, too, after an appeal to Maximilian as overlord of this area, a compromise agreement was reached in October 1508. The papal monopoly was recognized for two years, but the price of alum was lowered to almost half of what Chigi had asked at the time of the outbreak of the conflict.[64]

The import of alum from Asia Minor into England or the Low Countries met with difficulties because of the long sea route, and Turkish alum could be shipped to Venice more easily. This was significant not only because of the wealth of Venice but also because from Venice alum could be readily transported to the cloth-producing cities of southern Germany. Thus Venice was crucial in all attempts to make the monopoly of the Tolfa alum mines a reality. In the years before the War of the League of Cambrai, Rome sent one protest after another to Venice, remonstrating against the appearance of Turkish alum on the Venetian market—but to no avail.

The clashes in which Chigi became involved with various European governments showed that he pursued the opportunities inherent in the papal alum monopoly with greater energy and ruthlessness than previous tax farmers. Chigi was not the first lessee of the Tolfa mines, but he was more successful than his predecessors because he applied a remarkable—one is tempted to say modern—inventiveness to the reorganization of the work in the mines and to the sale of their product. Nevertheless, he could never have overcome all the difficulties if he had not had the full and continuous backing of Pope Julius II.

Actually, the person who issued the various protests and messages caused by infringement on the alum monopoly was not Chigi but the Pope. In the case of Venice, in November 1504 a

special papal emissary, Baptista Mauro, was sent with letters for
the papal nuncio, the Doge Loredan, and the Venetian patriarch.[65] The contents of the messages, complaining about the violation of the alum monopoly, were very much alike. The argument ran that the income from the Tolfa mines was destined for
the financing of crusades, and for support of those Christians
who had fled from Turkish rule to Italy. Those who sold, bought,
or used alum coming from Turkey, or those who transported it,
would be damned and excommunicated; the Turkish alum,
together with the ships that carried it, would be confiscated.
Since these admonitions had no effect, they were renewed in
February 1505. Similar messages of protest were sent to Venice
in the following September, when the news came to Rome that
Alvise Giustiniani and some other "sons of the Devil" (*perdi-
tionis filii*) had brought Turkish alum to Venice.

About the same time, in the fall of 1505, the Pope intervened
to prevent the use of Turkish alum in England.[66] Julius II first
turned to King Henry VII, asking him to prohibit the use of
Turkish alum in his realm. He also wrote directly to the captain
of the king's ship that he ought not sail to Asia Minor but should
get his alum in Civitavecchia from Chigi; but the captain, ignor-
ing the Pope's order, went back to England with Turkish alum.
Julius II now appealed in several letters to Henry VII, and even
to the king's mother, to prevent the sale of Turkish alum in England and to have it destroyed. In his letters to the king he referred not only to recent papal decrees establishing the Tolfa
monopoly, but referred back to the times of Innocent III and the
Fourth Lateran Council of 1215, with its prohibition of trade
with pagans. However, the Florentine firms of Frescobaldi and
Gualterotti continued to send Turkish alum to England, and in
May 1506 the Pope sent a special nuncio, Petrus Grifus, to England in order to discuss the "alum affair" with the king. Petrus
Grifus received a long instruction that, in every country through
which he traveled—Italy, France, Spain, Portugal, Flanders—he
ought to announce that those who sold or bought Turkish alum

would be excommunicated, and he should tell all archbishops and clerics to announce in all their churches the punishment for those who violated the papal edict. The Pope gave additional support to the mission by asking the collector of papal taxes in England, Polydore Virgil, to smooth Grifus' way. It is interesting that Petrus Grifus was not only papal nuncio but also a representative of the Chigi firm. His mission was unsuccessful, and he was called back.

Now Francesco Tommasi, Chigi's partner, went to England, and he succeeded in achieving the arrangement previously described. A particular target of papal ire in the correspondence with the English king had been the Florentine firm of Frescobaldi and Gualterotti. Their fault was not only that they bought Turkish alum for England; a good amount of this alum was sent on from England to the Low Countries, the most important market in northern Europe. England and France together used only half of the amount of alum which the Low Countries absorbed.[67] When Chigi's price rises had led to encouragement of the import of Turkish alum into the Low Countries, the Roman reaction was particularly sharp. In an encyclical dated June 17, 1506, Julius II solemnly confirmed the bull of Paul II of 1465 which had established the papal alum monopoly.[68] Julius' encyclical was addressed to the archbishops and bishops in Italy, France, Spain, Portugal and Germany, and even to the abbots of the chief religious orders. The importance of this encyclical was underlined by the fact that it was printed, and that the papal representative handed a copy personally to each of the importers of Turkish alum resident in Bruges. It reflects the strength of the position of the merchants in the Low Countries, and the crucial importance of this market for the alum trade, that negotiations resulted in the agreement which, as we have seen, was relatively favorable to the merchants.

Previous popes had issued declarations commanding observation of the Tolfa monopoly, but they had never raised the demand with such emphasis and pertinacity as Julius II. It might be said that the outcome did not correspond to the efforts that had been made. The agreements with England and Flanders were temporary and involved concessions with regard to amount and price. But the issue can be considered from a somewhat different angle. We should not forget that Chigi's lease of the Tolfa mines was for a limited time only; he was certainly more interested in drawing profits from them in the near future than in holding out for a long-term agreement which, even if it was obtained, might be of no use to him. The Pope, on the other hand, received from two important governments official recognition of his alum monopoly—certainly a strengthening of his legal position in the case of future difficulties and negotiations. Moreover, it was an implicit acknowledgment of the claim that the popes were the leaders of the Res Publica Christiana against threats from abroad. Undoubtedly Julius II and Chigi had been aware that, by acting together in this cause, they were serving their reciprocal interests; they had cooperated on each step to be taken.[69]

There were other indications of the closeness of the relations between Julius II and Agostino Chigi during these years. Chigi received favors and honors that were a clear sign of the Pope's confidence. In the Church of Santa Maria del Popolo, where several members of the Rovere family were buried, Chigi acquired a chapel as a burying place for his family. At his request Julius issued on December 3, 1507, a bull ordering a change of the saints to whom the chapel was dedicated. The saints venerated in this chapel before it was acquired by Chigi were Sigismund, Sebastian, and Rochus. Chigi declared that he had a special veneration for the Madonna of Loreto and of course for his name saint, Augustine, so the chapel was now rededicated to the Madonna of Loreto, to St. Augustine, and to St. Sebastian.[70] This favor was then followed in 1509 by a bull that made Agostino Chigi, his brothers, and their descendants members of the Rovere family and gave them the right, still used by their descendants, to call themselves "Chigi della Rovere."[71]

It was appropriate to the position he had achieved in Rome

that Chigi was no longer satisfied to live above his business office in the street where most of the other bankers had their offices and homes. He commissioned the best-known architects and painters of the time to construct and decorate a villa in the vineyards on the far side of the Tiber.[72] It was near completion when Chigi visited Venice in 1511, and the relations of pope and banker were such that the Pope, having returned to Rome while Chigi was still absent, was eager to visit the building site and to inspect what progress had been made.

JULIUS II in his rigorous defense of the alum monopoly of the Tolfa mines acted within the general program of his policy: to restore the papacy to full possession of its rights. That he was driven by this ambition has been frequently stated, and it is also agreed that, despite all the defects of his character and the questionable methods of his policy, this aim assures him a place as one of the great figures on the papal throne. One point that has been overlooked, however, is that Julius gave special attention to economic issues and to the assertion of papal rights in the economic field. His concern with the maintenance of the alum monopoly was not a unique case. On various occasions economic rights and claims emerged as motives for his foreign policy.

In the early years of the War of the League of Cambrai, the peace negotiations with Venice and the conflict leading to war with the Duke of Ferrara revealed the significance of economic issues in Julius's policy. When in July 1509, after long and humiliating delays because of the Pope's refusal to see the Venetian ambassadors who were sent to ask for absolution and peace, the negotiations got underway, it became known that one condition was unhindered navigation (*mare liberum*) on the "gulf," the Adriatic Sea, to all inhabitants of the papal states.[73] At the end of August the Venetian ambassadors, still excommunicated and not admitted to the presence of the Pope, persuaded Cardinal

Grimani, Antonio's son, to plead the cause of Venice before Julius II. The Pope was unwilling to relent in his demands. He even extended his demands regarding the gulf, saying that the Adriatic ought to be free to all Christian nations.[74] Two months later in a conversation with Francesco Corner, a Venetian diplomat who on his journey from Spain passed through Rome and who was an old friend of the Pope, Julius now officially informed the Venetians of his demand for *mare liberum* in the entire Adriatic. This came as a shock to the Venetian ambassadors and the government.[75] They believed that exclusive control over the Adriatic Sea was one of the foundations of Venetian wealth and power.

Actually the gulf is only the northern part of the Adriatic Sea, the waters north of a line running from Ancona to Zara. No warships of a non-Venetian power were permitted to enter this area, and ships carrying merchandise were forced to land in Venice and to pay tolls and duties before the goods could be transported to their ultimate destination. Venetian ships were stationed at the mouth of the rivers flowing into the Adriatic, and frequent inspections of the larger harbor towns guaranteed the strict enforcement of the Venetian claims. The strength of the Venetian fleet, the Venetian possessions along the entire eastern shore of the Adriatic, and the impossibility of reaching the more fertile and richer areas north of the Ancona-Zara line had the effect that, in practice, not only the gulf but the entire Adriatic was a Venetian sea.[76] The Venetian ambassadors in Rome and the Venetian cardinals at the Curia—Grimani and Corner—made desperate efforts to persuade the Pope to drop his demand. They stated that Venetian control of the Adriatic was in the general interest because it kept pirates and Turks away from Italy. They referred to the privileges that Pope Alexander III had granted to Venice during his struggle with Frederic Barbarossa in recognition of Venetian support. Alexander III had given Venice jurisdiction over the gulf; every year on the day of Assumption Venice commemorated this event in a celebration that was both secular and religious. The patriarch himself sanctioned the wedding of Venice with the sea, throwing a ring into the water with the words: "In signum suoi perpetuique dominii." As another proof of the Venetian right to jurisdiction over the gulf, the Venetian diplomats adduced that, according to Biondo, whom they characterized as a most reliable historian, the Council of Lyons in 1264 had given approval to Venice's arrangements with Ancona, and this implied recognition of the Venetian control of the gulf.[77]

Still the Pope could not be moved. The six galleys that at the beginning of the year the Pope had ordered to be built at Ancona, and which were now almost ready for service, would be of greater value than the Venetian ships.[78] Julius was adamant in his denial that previous popes could ever have made agreements that prevented their own subjects from sailing on the Adriatic Sea. But at the end, Julius II made a concession. He desisted from the demand that navigation on the gulf be entirely free: it would be free only for subjects of the papal states and ships sailing under the papal flag.[79]

Why was the Pope so eager to have a clause about free navigation in the Adriatic included in the peace treaty? The Venetians had some reasons to be surprised by this demand. When, at the beginning of the war, the pope had issued an edict in which he had explained the reasons for his action against Venice,[80] he listed numerous complaints: Venice's occupation of territory of the papal states, the Venetians' claims to tax the clergy at Venice, the Venetian custom to determine appointments to bishoprics in the area under Venetian control—but the question of *mare liberum* in the Adriatic had not been mentioned. Why did the Pope raise this demand now?[81] The Venetian diplomats speculated that Cardinal Soderini, the brother of the Florentine Gonfaloniere, was a driving force behind the demand because the Florentines were eager to shorten their trade route to the East by passing through the Adriatic.[82] But the fact that, at the end, the Pope was content with attaining freedom of navigation for his own ships suggests that there was not much substance in these Venetian speculations about the influence of Soderini. Probably the inhabitants of Ancona were agitating for lifting the restrictions imposed by Venice on their trade.[83] Such local interests, however, were certainly only a minor factor in the Pope's design.

Julius II, as Bembo has said, delighted in sea voyages.[84] He took an active interest in strengthening the defenses of the harbor of Civitavecchia; he created the nucleus of a fleet in Ancona. Chigi, as we have seen, built his own ships in Porto Ercole. The conclusion can be drawn that, like Chigi, the Pope too was eager to be free of dependence on Genoese and Venetian ships. Also, free navigation in the gulf would make it possible to transport alum directly into regions under control of the German king. Certainly, economic independence and sovereignty, at least for the papal states, formed part of Julius' vision of the restored power of the Church. It is tempting to assume that Chigi played some part in giving concrete content to that vision.

This is less speculative than it might appear because economic concerns also entered into the Pope's conflict with Ferrara, which followed almost immediately upon the settlement the Pope had forced on Venice. Here Chigi was certainly involved. Cervia was one of the towns that Venice had to return to the Pope after the fall of Cesare Borgia. It was one of the most important salt-producing areas in Italy. Nearby was another important source of salt—Comacchio, which was under the rule of the Duke of Ferrara. As long as Venice had Cervia, agreement with Ferrara restrained salt production in Comacchio, but after Cervia's surrender to the Pope, the Duke of Ferrara planned to make use of Comacchio's salt. He feared, however, that the Pope—as Ferrara's overlord—would try to prevent this. During the peace negotiations with Venice, therefore, the duke, Alfonso d'Este, asserted that he had received Comacchio as a fief from an emperor not from a pope.[85] This aroused the indignation of Julius, who asked the Venetian ambassadors for information about agreements that existed between Venice and Ferrara.[86]

Duke Alfonso defied the Pope's order to stop salt production at Comacchio and, indeed, made an agreement with France to provide Milan and French-occupied northern Italy with salt from Comacchio.

Certainly the clash over salt was not the decisive reason for the break between the pope and the Duke of Ferrara. Julius II was furious because of the obstacles Ferrara placed in the way of his plans to drive the French out of Italy. The duke not only refused to abandon his French alliance, but he also continued military operations against the Venetians, the Pope's new allies against France.[87] But the salt monopoly of Cervia was of importance in exacerbating the conflict, and the Comacchio arrangement was one of the main points of accusation in the papal bull that excommunicated Alfonso d'Este.[88] The bull stated that the duke had undertaken his work "in contempt of the papal decree, to the great damage of the Roman Church." The duke had been impertinent enough to deny the rights of the Church and further damaged them not only by increasing the duties on the import of salt into the dukedom, but by obligating himself to provide Milan with salt. He had rejected the fatherly admonitions of the Pope to desist from the pursuit of illegal gains and to listen to his conscience. His behavior in this case was that of an ungrateful son obstinately following an inclination toward treason and rebellion.

Why did Julius II give such weight to this issue? The Pope regarded Ferrara as a dangerous French outpost in the heart of Italy, and he was anxious to find as many counts of indictment as possible against the duke. We have contemporary testimony about the manner in which the Pope's attention was directed to the issue of the competition between the salt of Comacchio and the salt of Cervia.[89] "The following is the cause of his war," Luigi da Porto wrote to Antonio Savorgnano in 1511. "Alfonso d'Este, Duke of Ferrara, had decided to increase the salt production at Comacchio, and the Pope did the same or at least produced a great quantity in Cervia. He became aware that the duke had agreed with the King of France to provide salt for Lombardy, and at a much lower price than he had paid in the past. When this became known to Agostino Chigi, the wealthiest merchant in Italy, who had leased not only the alum mines but also the salt mines of the papal state,[90] he complained to the Pope, explaining to him that the Church would suffer much damage from such an agreement because, if the salt of Cervia could no longer be sold in Lombardy, the lease of the salt mines could no longer bring the price that he paid now. Moreover, if the duke could sell the salt for whatever he wanted, and send it to any place he wanted, many people in Tuscany and the Romagna would buy the salt cheaper from Comacchio." Two years later, after the withdrawal of the French from Italy, the Duke of Ferrara went to Rome to ask Julius II for peace and forgiveness. He left as regent in Ferrara his brother, Cardinal Ippolito d'Este. In order to secure the duke a favorable reception at the papal court, Ippolito ordered the salt mines of Comacchio to be destroyed.[91]

This indicates that economic interests weighed heavily with Julius II in his conduct of foreign policy and that he deliberated on these questions with Chigi. So let us take another look at the events described at the beginning of this book: Chigi's negotiations in Venice in the first half of 1511. In terms of chronology, they followed close the episodes just mentioned: the disputes over the sale of alum in the Low Countries, the Pope's demand for transforming the Adriatic Sea into a *mare liberum*, and his insistence on the salt monopoly of Cervia. Of course, the direct impetus for Chigi's trip to Venice came from his personal business interests. He hoped to obtain payment of debts and was anxious to investigate some fraudulent proceedings that had occurred in his Venetian agency.[92] Nevertheless, because of the close relationship between Julius II and Chigi—perhaps still more, because of the political situation at the time of Chigi's mission—it seems likely that Chigi's trip was also inspired by political considerations and that it was connected with papal policy.

This answer to the central question of motive is almost forced on us by a fact that previous writers have never mentioned: before Chigi went to Venice, he stayed in Bologna. This is significant because Julius II was also in Bologna. The Pope had left Rome for that city in August 1510 in order to supervise and accelerate the military operations against the Duke of Ferrara and his French allies. Chigi followed the Pope to Bologna, as his letters to his brother Sigismondo[93] show, and he stayed for a while in the Pope's suite. It is unimaginable that Chigi's trip to Venice was undertaken without intensive prior consultation with the Pope.

When, in 1509, the Pope started peace negotiations with Venice, he was alarmed by the growth of French power in northern Italy, as we have seen. He was willing to make peace with Venice because he wanted to have Venetian support in a war against France.[94] But Julius II was also aware that the surest means of halting the rise of French power would be to turn Maximilian, the German king, away from his French alliance and to bring him into the war against France.[95] Maximilian might be enticed to reverse alliances if he were given the towns of the terra firma that before the war had been ruled by Venice but that he regarded as belonging to Austria and the German empire. Since Maximilian was in constant financial straits, he might also be influenced toward a change of sides by a considerable payment of money. In the Pope's view, a settlement with Venice had not only the advantage of gaining an ally against France but also of giving the Pope the possibility of acting as mediator between Venice and Maximilian: he could try to convince the Venetians of the necessity of making certain concessions to Maximilian: territorial or financial concessions, or a mixture of both—to cede to Maximilian some of the towns on the terra firma and to pay tribute for those remaining under Venetian control.

Peace between the Pope and Venice was concluded in February 1510, but military operations in the spring and summer of 1510 did not leave much room for further diplomatic maneuvering. In the last months of 1510 and the beginning of 1511, the situation seemed stable enough for a new diplomatic initiative, and the Pope felt encouraged to make another attempt to bring the Venetians and Maximilian together. Julius II, who frequently complained about the lack of energy in the Venetian war effort, knew about the financial straits of the Venetian government; he may even have feared that, in desperation, the Venetians might throw themselves into the arms of the French king.[96] It seemed most desirable, therefore, to lighten their burden and to infuse some energy into the Venetian preparations for the summer campaign of 1511.

On the other hand, after the unfortunate campaign of summer 1510, the prospects of a new effort in the same political constellation were not very encouraging. The Venetian government might now be ready, therefore, to make Maximilian those concessions that would induce him to abandon the French alliance. Negotiations with Maximilian were underway, and there was some reason to hope that he might change sides; he was sending his confidant Mathaeus Lang, the Bishop of Gurk, to Italy with peace proposals.[97] There seemed to be manifold advantages in giving Venice some financial support—to spur the Venetian military effort and to weaken the resistance against concessions to Maximilian.

THIS, then, was the situation when Chigi came to Venice, and it is altogether likely that these considerations were discussed by Julius II and Chigi in Bologna in the months before. We know that political issues were not the only ones that brought Chigi to Venice. The penetration of Turkish alum through Venice into the European market was a very serious concern. An alliance between Venice and the Pope must have appeared to Chigi as a great opportunity to plug the hole in his alum monopoly. From the beginning of his career at the Roman Curia, Chigi was aware of the dependence of the businessman on the ruler. The Pope had granted Chigi the rights that formed the foundation of his wealth: the tax farming of the Tolfa mines. Chigi had needed papal backing for maintaining the alum monopoly in England and the Low Countries, and these negotiations were fresh in his mind. In the case of the peace with Venice and the clash with Ferrara, the interconnection between politics and business had been forcefully demonstrated. The parallel of the Pope's interests and his own was evident. It can be concluded that Chigi's journey to Venice had a double motivation: politics and business.

This interpretation of Chigi's presence in Venice throws additional light on why he finally concluded his negotiations in August 1511. Maximilian and the Pope could not come to an understanding in the early spring of 1511, and the military disasters of the armies of the Pope and the Venetians in the same spring and early summer made Chigi reluctant to give final approval to the arrangements with Venice. But, by July, the Pope saw new prospects of forming an anti-French coalition. Venice, on the flank of the French and barring the advance of the Germans, emerged once again as an important factor in papal strategy. Julius was anxious that Venice should not limit its efforts to regaining lost territory on the terra firma; the papal and Venetian armies should become a united force, "driving the barbarians out of Italy." The so-called Holy League provided for a commander-in-chief who would be paid in equal parts by the Pope and Venice, each of them contributing 20,000 ducats monthly. Now a loan to Venice might again be of decisive importance, since it would ease the acceptance of the arrangements and would take care, at least, of the first payment to the new commander-in-chief. Thus Chigi was now willing to complete the contract, which he had negotiated since March. It was fitting that when on October 4, 1511, the instrument establishing the Holy League was signed, Agostino Chigi's name appeared as witness.[98]

---◦⋇{ V }⋇◦---

The Closing
of the Account

I N HIS LAST WILL, which he set up in August 1519, Agostino
Chigi left the house, garden, and stables he had built in Rome
on the other side of the Tiber, in Trastevere, to his sons and their
male descendants, with the condition that they were not to mort-
gage the property or let it out of their hands.[1] If the male descendants of Agostino's sons died out, the house was to go to the
male descendants of his brother Sigismondo, under the same
conditions, and if Sigismondo's male descendants died out, it
would go to the male descendants of Agostino's younger brother
Francesco. Only if there were no male descendants of any of his
brothers could the house come into the possession of the male
descendents of Agostino's eldest daughter.

The purpose of the testament is clear: Chigi had many other
houses and possessions, but his Villa Suburbina—as contemporaries called the house in Trastevere—was meant to be the family
seat, the center of the Chigi family. Chigi's arrangements—
short-lived as they were because, even before the sixteenth century ended, Chigi's legal conditions were set aside and the villa
was sold to the Farnese, becoming the Villa Farnesina—suggested that he felt sure he had raised the Chigis to the rank of the
great Roman families and that he wanted all the Chigis to be
aware that he, Agostino, was the founder of the family fortunes.

Anyone who entered the villa became immediately aware of
Chigi's pride and hopes, for praise of Agostino was built into it.
Painted in the center of the ceiling of the garden loggia is the figure of Fame blowing a great trumpet.[2] There can be no doubt
whose fame this figure is meant to spread around the world. The

central paintings are surrounded by a number of small paintings showing signs of the Zodiac and of planetary gods, together with figures of classical mythology whose stories are related to the symbols of the planets. All these scenes show the constellation of the stars at the time of Chigi's birth on December 1, 1466: the paintings on the ceiling of the loggia represent his horoscope.

The belief that the constellation of the stars at the hour of a man's birth indicates the lines along which his life will develop was common in the Renaissance.[3] As a merchant whose ships were tossed by winds and storms and whose affairs involved incalculable risks, Chigi was perhaps even more aware than others of the power of Fortuna—of the domination of life by forces beyond human control. But it should not be overlooked that the representation of the Zodiac and the planets on the ceiling of his villa are also associated with ancient gods and heroes, symbolizing an abundance of man's potentialities: inventiveness, cleverness, strength, passion, artistic creativity. Chigi shared the admiration of his humanistic age for the classical world, and he must have learned from the ancients that the powers inherent in man's nature, his virtù, were requisite to man's achievements. As a young man Chigi recommended that his father employ Pinturicchio for work in Siena.[4] In later years, he must have frequently seen on the floor of the cathedral a graffito that Pinturicchio had drafted, showing the Fortuna's power was limited, that Fortuna could bring men only to the point at which they would have to demonstrate their virtù through their own ability. In Chigi's time people disputed passionately whether you could rely on your own strength, whether everything depended on making use of the opportunities which Fortuna threw your way, or whether all that happened had been written in the stars. But Chigi did not choose among these explanations of human affairs—he saw them coming together to shape a man's life.

Chigi's life and career certainly must have been conducive to such a dual attitude: confidence in man's power and recognition of forces outside man. His contemporaries believed that Chigi applied to his business affairs an almost uncanny cleverness; he made use of every economic advantage or legal lacuna. He was proud of what he had achieved by his own efforts. At the same time, however, Chigi was always aware of the need to be backed by the rulers of his time. Julius II was always the superior whose orders he carried out. The Petrucci ruler of Siena to whom Chigi was closely related he treated with deep respect, almost subservience. Throughout 1511, Chigi negotiated with the Gonzaga family about the possibility of marrying a natural daughter of the Gonzaga ruler of Mantua.[5] The project failed because even Chigi's wealth could not overcome the resistance of the lady, but her father, the Marquess of Mantua, had favored the plan. His only condition was that Chigi should abandon his business life and convert his money into land. Interstingly enough, Chigi was willing to accept this condition. Unlike the Florentine or Venetian patricians who, living in republics, thought themselves at least equal to the rulers of the many Italian states, Chigi, born in the Siena of the Petruccis and living as an adult in papal Rome, lived in a world of courts and princes and was imbued with the notions of a social hierarchy, a world divided into few rulers and many ruled. Although he was certainly aware that even among the rulers there was a hierarchy and he could not aspire to reach the top, he wanted his family to have a place within the world of rulers. To be a merchant was an instrument for such an ascent, not a value in itself.

The nature of Chigi's financial activities contributed to his ambition. The basis of his great wealth was a lease that depended on papal favor and was limited in time. He was a banker who made his money work by advancing loans or in companies formed to make use of particular opportunities. There was in Rome no Monte in which to invest money; nor were the Chigis owners or partners in an ancient manufacturing enterprise. For Chigi, the accessible investments for the preservation of wealth were houses, land, jewels, tapestries. These possessions promised to have a permanent value and to raise his family into the ruling nobility.

In the era of Julius II, Chigi was involved in politics and had an influential role. After Julius' death, in the time of Leo X, Chigi is mentioned mainly as one of the outstanding figures of the brilliant society of Medicean Rome. He is the great patron of the artists for whom Bramante, Raphael, Peruzzi, Giulio Romano, Sebastiano del Piombo, and Sodoma worked.[6] He financed a printing press, which in 1515 published a Greek Pindar.[7] One also wonders whether, when he employed the poet Aretino as clerk in his bank, he was not influenced by the young man's literary interests and gifts.[8] The banquets Chigi gave for the Pope and visiting princes were famous for their magnificence; ambassadors reported about them to their governments with admiration tinted by only a little disgust.[9] These were the feasts of which it was told that after each course the silver from which the guests had eaten was thrown into the Tiber. It was also said that Chigi ordered nets placed below the surface of the water so that fishermen could collect the silver and return it to him the next morning.

But while we hear about the splendor of Chigi's life and household in the Rome of Leo X, we hear much less about his financial activities. Certainly, he loaned large sums to the Pope, beginning with Leo's coronation.[10] The granting of this loan guaranteed Chigi and his associates another twelve-year lease to the Tolfa mines after the original lease expired in 1513, the first year of Leo's reign. Certainly financial support of the Pope was indispensable to Chigi's position, but there is no indication that he pursued his business interests with the same energy as in the days of Julius II. Actually, the chief tax farmer of the Tolfa mines in 1513 was not Agostino Chigi but another Sienese, Andrea Bellanti, and Chigi was only a partner with a 20 percent share.[11] Still it is assumed that Chigi remained the dominating figure in the enterprise, and shortly before his death he again became chief farmer of the mines.[12] Although Chigi did not abandon his business activities under Leo X, it is evident that he did not want to spend all his time on them: the image he wanted to convey was not that of a businessman but of a leading figure of Roman society.

The acme of this part of Chigi's career was reached on August 28, 1519, the day of his name saint, St. Augustine. On this day Chigi signed his last will and testament, and the act was witnessed by fourteen cardinals and other high clerics.[13] Not only this, but the witnesses also attended a ceremony that preceded the reading of the will: Chigi's wedding to Francesca Ordeaschi, whom he had brought to Rome from Venice eight years before and by whom he had four children. The wedding took place in Chigi's Villa Suburbina, and Pope Leo X himself placed the rings on the fingers of the couple.

W HEN A LETTER from Rome reporting Chigi's wedding reached Venice, Sanudo noted the fact in his diary and he was shocked.[14] It seemed inappropriate to him that the Pope should be present at the wedding of a man who had had four children with the woman he was only then getting around to marrying. Moreover, she was the daughter of a poor Venetian grocer.[15] A month later, in an instruction to Marco Minio, the Venetian ambassador in Rome, the Venetian government called Chigi "a suspicious and deceptive person."[16]

This attack on Chigi is rather surprising when we think back to August 1511 and the honors that the Venetian government granted him, and remember the respect with which he was treated by the leading men of the republic. But since then, the relations between Chigi and the Venetian government had been on a rocky course. In the late summer of 1519, there was a bitter struggle going on. The matter under dispute was still the now old issue: the Venetian government had not yet repaid the 20,000 ducats it had borrowed from Chigi in 1511, and Chigi still had the jewels from San Marco which had been given as security for the loan. Although eight years had passed since the conclusion of the contract, no settlement had been reached. Actually the negotiations in 1519 that led to the testy outburst just quoted were already the second attempt to solve the problem. The first was made in the course of the year following the agreement of August 1511.

When in that August Chigi sailed from Venice, he left with the Venetian government a memorandum in which he said that he would lend the Venetian government 20,000 ducats immediately; the Venetian government could have six months—until early January 1512—to decide whether it wanted to go ahead with the other part of the bargain, the sale of alum.[17] If in January 1512, the 20,000 ducats would be returned to Chigi, the entire contract would be null and void. By the end of 1511, there was a strong feeling in Venice among the members of the Council of Ten, as well as in the Pregadi, that it might be best to terminate the contract because it would bind Venice too firmly to Rome. Just then, the Pope was again anxious to separate the German king from his French alliance and tried to lure him away by offering him territories in the terra firma. Yet, although it might be advantageous to get rid of the tie to Rome and Chigi, obviously repayment of the debt would require the raising of new taxes.[18] Consequently, after deliberations in the Council of Ten and in the Pregadi, in which there was agreement about the desirability of repaying Chigi his loan, the Council of Savi suggested to the Pregadi the imposition of a decima for the purpose of terminating the contract with Chigi. But Grimani, Leonardo Mocenigo, and Giogio Emo—all three advocates of the agreement with Chigi—proposed that the decision on this issue should be postponed, and this was accepted. Priuli commented bitterly that always when new taxes were proposed immediately the counter-proposal was made to postpone the decision. The unwillingness of the Venetians to impose new taxes meant that the contract with Chigi was now in force. Venice agreed to buy the 7000 cantari of alum, but expected to resell them immediately to Alessandro Schiapi under the conditions established in May.

Now there was a new turn of affairs. Schiapi was neither willing nor able to carry out his part of the bargain within the prescribed period, that is, between January and April 1512. The Venetian government informed Chigi of Schiapi's refusal and asked Chigi to do what he had promised: find a buyer in case the deal with Schiapi could not be consummated. A new agreement that both prolonged and revised the previous arrangement was signed on July 19, 1512. Chigi was given more time—eight months beginning in August 1512—to find a buyer for the alum. Venice, for its part, gained chance to terminate the contract if within the next six months it repaid Chigi the 20,000 ducats. There was one further condition: as long as Venice remained in Chigi's debt, he could sell alum to Venice at the high price of 20 ducats and would have to pay only half of the customary import duty. Moreover, the government guaranteed him that only his alum would be sold on the Venetian market.[19]

According to the revised agreement, the deadline for final settlement was the spring of 1513. Yet for a long period the documents are silent about the affair. This was a time of great instability and change on the political scene: Julius II died on February 21, 1513. First it was uncertain who would be his successor and, when Leo X was elected, the question was what his policy would be. Venice had turned from the papal to the French side with unfortunate results. The victory of the Swiss at Novara in June 1513 again brought enemies as close to Venice as they had been in 1509 and 1511. For Venice, this was certainly not the time to use its resources for the repayment of a loan. Chigi too cannot have thought this the right moment to make further investments in Venice. For both parties the maintenance of the existing situation had advantages: for Venice, the negative advantage that it did not have to repay the loan or enter on a gradual repayment schedule; for Chigi, the positive advantage that the Venetian market remained reserved for the alum from Tolfa and he could sell it there at a high price. Chigi seems to have had some doubts whether the Venetians kept strictly to the agreement. He believed that alum from other sources might have entered the Venetian market, and twice, in 1514 and 1517, he made remonstrations to the Venetian government.[20] But we hear nothing about negotiations to terminate the agreement before the spring of 1519.

By 1519, the political situation had completely changed; the war had ended. For Venice the final act was the reentry of Venetian troops under Gritti into Verona on January 24, 1517. Andrea Mocenigo, a Venetian patrician, began to write a history of the War of the League of Cambrai while the fighting was going on. The last sentences of this work were written on August 13, 1517, and the event with which he ended was the restoration of Venetian rule to Verona.[21] He describes the joy of the inhabitants at the victory of their old rulers. In processions they carried gilded lions of San Marco bearing the words: "Truth again lives on earth and has brought down justice from heaven." He then briefly referred to the sacrifices that Venice had made in this war. The expenses were immense and how these sums were collected "is a marvelous thing accomplished by no other republic." One of the means had been the sale of offices, but now that the danger was over, the Senate had decreed that no one could buy honors; they must be earned by virtue.[22]

Mocenigo compared the achievements of the Venetian Republic with those of the most famous republics of the ancient world. Although the deeds of the Athenians and the Romans were certainly magnificent, at no time in their history did they have to contend with so many kings as Venice had. The theme that Venice was the one state of modern times in which the virtues and wisdom of the ancient world were still alive is also taken up in various Venetian writings on history and politics.[23] Egnazio, friend of many patricians and associate of Aldus, wrote a book comparing the great figures of Venetian history with those of the ancient world—a comparison that did not turn out to the Venetians' disadvantage. Contarini's famous book on the Venetian Republic argued that Venice was the ideal republic which ancient philosophers imagined but which had never existed in the ancient world.

This idealization of Venetian policy had diverse motives: it was both defense and admonition. It served to obliterate the mistakes of the past by presenting the ruling class as heirs of traditional political wisdom, but it was also a warning against becoming spoiled by wealth and luxury, an appeal to return to ancestral virtues and discipline. Such an image of Venice was hardly compatible with the fact that Venice remained in debt to a Roman banker and that jewels from the treasury of San Marco were in the hands of a foreigner. Like the termination of the sale of offices, the freeing of Venice from the dependence on Chigi was needed to show that Venice had regained its old power. Certainly the complaints of merchants about the high price they had to pay for alum lent the issue practical urgency. There were various reasons, therefore, why on April 27, 1519, the Council of Ten decided that it was time to ask Chigi to return the jewels he had received as security for the loan.[24]

SINCE CHIGI was a private businessman, the Venetian government decided to approach him in an unofficial, informal manner. Giorgio Corner wrote to his son, the cardinal in Rome, to arrange the return of the jewelry for repayment of the loan; on May 17, 1519, the government gave Cardinal Corner the necessary powers of attorney.[25] At the beginning the discussions with Chigi proceeded smoothly and rapidly; but in a letter from the Cardinal, dated June 24, came an inkling that difficulties might be ahead. Chigi wanted his right to sell alum in Venice prolonged for one year.[26] The Venetian government took no notice of Chigi's request but went ahead and sent an expert to examine the jewelry. He found it in good order, although the chief piece, a large necklace, imitating the upper part of a knight's mailed shirt and consisting of rubies, diamonds, and pearls, was broken in two parts.[27] A new power of attorney was given to Cardinal Corner, which entitled him to give Chigi 20,000 ducats and to take the jewelry into custody. However, the Venetian government now seemed to feel that it could not entirely disregard Chigi's request for prolongation of his alum monopoly and so made the offer that, until the ratification of a final agreement, Venice would prohibit the import of other alum and Chigi would not be asked to pay additional duties on the alum he had already brought into Venice.[28] Corner now gave Chigi 20,000 ducats and Chigi handed over to him the jewelry, which the Cardinal was to hold until ratification of the agreement.

Chigi now set up the final text of the agreement that he wanted the Venetian government to ratify, and on August 9, 1519, Cardinal Corner sent it to Venice.[29] This document transformed the negotiations between Chigi and the Venetian government into a sharp controversy, which lasted almost until Chigi's death in the spring of 1520. The conflict involved the services of the best Roman lawyers, confiscation of property, and excommunication and intervention by Pope Leo X. When Corner sent the document to Venice, he remarked that the Venetians ought to take a close look at it.[30] The Venetians were shocked, indeed, when they did. It seemed to them so long and burdensome, with so many clauses, terms, and revisions, that "they had become rather concerned; they were not used to defraud anyone but they also did not like to be deceived or outwitted." The demand that upset them most was that Chigi not only asked for forty days during which he could sell alum in Venice without having to pay additional taxes, but he wanted to be protected against all possible damages that his or his employees' goods might suffer; for this he demanded a security of 10,000 ducats. The Venetians feared that this clause would lead to endless litigation, and during the time of litigation the security would be in Chigi's hands: he would be richer by 10,000 ducats.

104

The Venetian councils met several times to discuss Chigi's demand and wavered in their views about how to respond. First they looked for a formula that might diminish the possibility of litigation,[31] but they then decided on a less accommodating line.[32] In their instructions to Cardinal Corner, they said that they were very upset by Chigi's using words which indicated that he did not know "the rectitude and legality of the Venetian government." Nevertheless, they were willing to make a final offer. The Cardinal ought to tell Chigi that he could keep all the profits he had made from the sale of alum in the past, that there would be no additional taxes or imposition for alum already brought into Venice, and that in the future he would be permitted to sell alum in Venice at the going price. About all other issues arising from the negotiations in 1511, there would be "perpetual silence"—this meant they would not raise the accusation of usury. But if Chigi again proved to be obstructive and refused agreement, then the cardinal ought to return the jewels to him, and he should ask Chigi to give back the 20,000 ducats. They also told the Cardinal that, in order to force a decision, they had sequestered all the alum Chigi had stored in Venice and had blocked all payments to Chigi's agent, Raphael Besalù, to whom Venetians were believed to owe something like 20,000 ducats.

The Venetians, who had some experience in negotiating with Chigi, ought not to have been so astonished when he reacted angrily to Venice's harsh measure of confiscation. He made use of the clauses in the contract of 1511 that all disputes arising out of the contract ought to be decided before a papal tribunal; he asked the Rota to excommunicate the fifty Venetians who had given him pledges of security because they had violated their vows.[33] On receiving this information, the Venetian ambassador rode in heavy rain over swampy roads to the Pope's hunting lodge to stay the execution of the excommunication. Now Cardinal Corner and Chigi were ordered to appear before the Pope, and this resulted in an altercation in the presence of the Pope. Leo tried to be as Solomonic as possible and suggested a simple document, stating nothing but the fact that Chigi had received the money and that Corner ought to keep the jewels until the litigation was decided. The Pope declared his willingness to stay the excommunication of the fifty Venetians until then.

The Venetians were clearly frustrated by this course of events but could only agree to drawing up a document in accordance with the Pope's decisions. The money would be left with Chigi and the jewels with Cardinal Corner until the court had decided. But in order to avoid a long legal battle, they made one more attempt to come to an understanding with Chigi. They renewed their offer that he could sell the alum he had already imported into Venice at the price of 20 ducats, without having to pay additional duties. But they also prepared their ambassador in Rome for the coming legal fight, providing him with complete documentation of the entire affair, sending him legal opinions favorable to the Venetian cause, and telling him to seek the services of the best lawyers.[34]

Our reports about the debate in the Pregadi reveal the frustration and fury over the clever manner in which Chigi had maneuvered Venice into appearing to be in the wrong. One of the sharpest critics of Chigi was Antonio Grimani. One cannot help wondering whether he felt guilty because of his prominent role in arranging the old contract with Chigi and because he had helped make the pledges that now brought many of his colleagues under the cloud of excommunication. Was the vehemence with which he now attacked Chigi an expression of bad conscience? Luca Tron, one of the opponents of the contract in 1511, was unable to curb his tongue when he remarked that too much favor had been shown Chigi in the past.

At the request of the Council of Savi, the Pregadi approved a public proclamation stating that everyone who wanted to bring alum to Venice to sell could do so without paying the customary duties. Grimani also proposed that Cardinal Corner be asked to hand over to the Venetian ambassador in Rome the jewels that Chigi had given him. At this meeting of the Pregadi, on October

22, 1514, the views of legal experts who opposed measures inter-
fering in a suit before court prevailed. But one month later, Grimani's proposal was adopted. Cardinal Corner was sent a rather
peremptory request to hand over the jewels to the Venetian
ambassador; the cardinal refused. He had committed himself to
hand over the jewels to the Venetian government only after ratification of the agreement on the exchange of jewels and money,
and he had to keep his promise. So he returned the jewels to
Chigi, and Chigi returned the 20,000 ducats to the cardinal.[35]
Negotiations seemed to be at an end, and further steps would
have to wait for the court decision.

Then a sudden development took place that ushered in a new,
final stage in the long dispute about the contract of 1511. This
last negotiation clearly demonstrates the qualities that were so
crucial in Chigi's successful career: his cleverness and his tough-
ness. When the Venetian government initiated the negotiations
in the spring of 1519, Chigi had little to bargain with, but now
having brought in the Roman Curia, he was in a strong position.
At the end of December, a Roman gentleman—whose name is
never revealed—approached the Venetian ambassador and told
him that he came on behalf of Chigi. He understood that Chigi
would be willing to submit the entire litigation to final decision
by the Pope. This intermediary also revealed what Chigi's real
motive had been in raising one difficulty after another. Chigi
considered it unfair that for eight years the Venetians had at
their disposal 20,000 ducats and he had received no interest on
that loan. Chigi, of course, could argue that when the contract
was concluded in 1511, interest was included: it was to come
from the fictitious sale provided for in the agreement, and it consisted in the difference between the price that Venice paid for
alum and the lower price at which it would be resold to an employee of Chigi's. Because this part of the 1511 agreement had
never been carried out, Chigi maintained that he had given the
loan without receiving benefit from it.

The report about the conversations with the Roman gentleman produced excitement and much discussion in the Venetian government.[36] The Venetian's were in complete agreement that Chigi had not only fair but "excessive" benefits from his contract with Venice; he had earned 30-32,000 ducats more than he would have made at any other place from the high price of his alum. But the Venetians were in a quandary about Chigi's suggestion to submit the dispute to papal arbitration. To many it seemed unpolitic to refuse the Pope as arbitrator, but it was feared that because of his financial obligations to Chigi, Leo X might be inclined to favor him. Some therefore wanted to refuse the entire proposal out of hand; others felt that it would be better to explore what was behind the overtures of the Roman gentleman. It was decided to make a counter-proposal—to ask for arbitration by two judges and see whether this would lead to a resumption of negotiations.[37]

The Venetians were not disappointed. Negotiations got underway again,[38] but those who had expected smooth sailing were wrong. Chigi proved to be as tough as he had been in the past. Both parties now agreed that Chigi ought to get some compensation for having given a loan without interest. Chigi demanded, therefore, that the preferential treatment the Tolfa alum enjoyed on the Venetian market ought to be continued for another three years. The Venetian government wrote to Minio, their ambassador in Rome, that this demand changed the basis on which the negotiations had been resumed; what had then been mentioned was an extension of eighteen months. Rather indignantly, the Venetians wrote that whenever they showed a sign of agreeing to Chigi's demands, he retreated from what was "fair and right"; in consideration of the great profits he had made in Venice, it seemed entirely unjustified to allow Chigi to sell alum in Venice at privileged conditions for another three years. However, Venice was willing to make a final offer. Chigi might keep his monopoly for one further year. If Chigi again refused to accept, no further negotiations would take place, and the solution of the issue wuld have to wait for the decision of the courts.[39] Chigi neither accepted nor refused the final offer: he answered with the counter-proposal that his monopoly ought to last two years, not just one.[40] The two parties seemed close to agreement, and at the request of the Venetian ambassador, Chigi asked Leo X to lift the excommunication of the fifty Venetians.[41] But whether this meant that Chigi was now ready to conclude an accord, we will never know. Three weeks later, on April 11, he died.

O N APRIL 6, 1520, Raphael died, and Marc Antonio Michiel, an art-loving Venetian patrician who was in Rome in the entourage of the young Cardinal Pisani, wrote with deep emotion about the terrible loss the world had suffered. He added: "In my opinion, although the great mass of the people does not share my view, yesterday's death of Agostino Chigi will cause much less damage."[42] Michiel was right in stating that this was not how the world of Rome looked upon the banker's death. Agostino Chigi was buried in Santa Maria del Popolo with the greatest pomp.[43] The procession was led by members of the religious orders, followed by priests from all the Roman churches, and a large delegation of Sienese, all carrying tall wax candles. Chigi was embalmed, laid on a bier draped with gold brocade, his body covered with a cloak of black satin. Members of the households of the Pope and the cardinals, all the officials of the Curia, and many friends were in attendance—altogether about 5000 people.

The solemnity and ceremony with which Chigi was buried demonstrated his closeness to the rulers of the Roman Church. He was a court banker, one of the early and, at the same time, one of the most brilliant examples of a type that emerged in increasing numbers later in early modern Europe. Chigi himself, and this is testimony to his talents, did not experience the vagaries of dependence on the favors of the ruling powers. But after his death, when the backing of the papal court was no longer at the service of the Chigis, it became difficult for them to hold on to their claims and possessions. One month after Chigi's death, in May, the executors of his will made an agreement with the Venetian government which essentially corresponded to the last offer the Venetians had made when Chigi was still alive and to which he had not given his assent.[44] Sequestration of the alum Chigi had imported to Venice would be ended. The fifty Venetians who had been excommunicated would be absolved; the jewels would go back to the Venetian government, which paid Chigi's heirs 20,000 ducats; and the monopoly of the Tolfa alum would continue for another year during which a cantaro of alum could still be sold for 20 ducats. But a few months later, even this agreement was changed in Venice's favor: it was agreed that, for a payment of 2000 ducats, the preferential treatment given to Chigi's alum would terminate immediately. The Venetian archives contain no further mention of this business.

-- ❊❦ VI ❧❊ --

Julius II:
Caesar and Vicar of Christ

WHEN JULIUS II was forming his Holy League against France in the summer of 1511, Erasmus was supervising the printing of his most widely read work, *Praise of Folly*. In this witty and devastating attack on man's vanities, avarice, and ambitions, on his lack of reason, on his faith in worldly wisdom and his failure to recognize his true interests, two themes dominate: one is the Church's deviation from the ideals of its founders, that is, its involvement in secular affairs and its preoccupation with pomp and riches; the other is man's passion for power, his efforts to exert rule over others and to use violence for these ends. In condemning war Erasmus himself rather than Folly seems to speak: "War is so monstrous a thing that it befits beasts and not men, so violently insane that poets represent it as an evil visitation of the Furies, so pestilential that it causes a general corruption of character, so criminal that it is best waged by the worst men, and so impious that it has no relation with Christ."[1]

From his early years, Erasmus was vehemently opposed to war; his pacifism was strengthened by what he had seen and experienced during the three years he spent in Italy, from 1506 to 1509.[2] The war upset his plans and interfered with his scholarly pursuits. In Bologna, a center of military operations, the university functioned only irregularly; the University of Padua closed when the War of the League of Cambrai broke out; and Aldus, with whom Erasmus stayed in Venice, shut down his printing presses. After a few months in Rome, Erasmus found himself in the midst of a military and political crisis and he left the city. He was unable, therefore, to make use of the offer of Cardinal Gri-

111

mani to live in his palace and work in his library, which was rich in valuable codices. For the rest of his life Erasmus was bitter about having lost the opportunity to make his home in Rome and to enjoy "its bright light, the noble setting of the most famous city in the world, the delightful freedom, the many richly furnished libraries, the sweet society of all these great scholars, all the literary conversations, all the monuments of antiquity."[3]

To Erasmus, the man responsible for causing the unrest and destruction was the Pope, Julius II. In Bologna in 1506, Erasmus had watched the entry of Julius as Triumphator parading through the city. In 1509 Julius asked Erasmus whether the papacy should join the League against Venice.[4] But the Pope disregarded his advice to shy away from war and joined the conflict. For Erasmus Julius II became the embodiment of war and all its evils. In *Julius Exclusus*, composed after the Pope's death, Erasmus gave full vent to his fury,[5] and he gave expression to his hostile feelings in other writings as well. In a letter to Julius' successor, Leo X, for example, although he was more cautious in his formulation, Erasmus showed his deep dislike of Julius' policies: "Let others exalt the wars aroused by the energy of Julius II or fought by him to successful finish; let them tell of the victories won by his armies and recount the triumphs that he celebrated in such kingly style. Great as the glory might be that they will adjudge him, they must confess all the same that it meant misery for many people."[6] Erasmus' allusion to Julius' delight in triumphal processions certainly refers to what he had witnessed in Bologna—the contrast between the suffering caused by war and the undisguised enjoyment expressed in the splendor of a triumphant entry.

A S ERASMUS was composing *Praise of Folly*, Titian was working in Padua on a large woodcut entitled *The Triumph of Christ*.[7] It depicts a long procession, an "endless number of figures," as Vasari notes. At the head are Adam and Eve; after them come the heroes of Jewish history with Abraham brandishing his sword and Joshua holding high his helmet; the next group is formed by the Sibyls carrying banners that dance in the wind; then comes a cross-bearer followed by the chariot bearing Christ, which is drawn by the symbolic beasts of the Evangelists, aided by the four doctors of the Church. The figures following Christ are heroes of the history of the Christian era; outstanding among them are a gigantic Christopher and a St. George in dazzling armor. The last figures of the procession, which disappears behind a gate, are monks and holy women. The ideas of Titian's woodcut have many origins. The *trionfi* of Petrarch, the processions of fraternities and lay brotherhoods, Savonarola's *Triumphus Christi*, and Mantegna's *Triumph of Caesar* all provided models. But the political situation—the formation of the Holy League with the Pope at its head—may also have been a stimulus.

The combination of Christian and pagan elements in Titian's woodcut is particularly striking if one compares it with Savonarola's description of the triumph of Christ. In Savonarola's treatise Christ has a crown of thorns on his head; he shows the stigmata; he holds the Bible in his right hand and the cross and the instruments of his suffering in his left. In Titian's woodcut Christ's right hand shows stigmata but he carries only the sign of worldly domination, a scepter: Titian's Christ is a ruler returning after a victorious campaign as Triumphator to his realm.

These two works, Erasmus' *Praise of Folly* and Titian's *Triumph of Christ*, express contrasting views about the function of the Christian Church. According to Erasmus priests ought to model their lives after that of Christ and his disciples, and they ought to serve as an example for all Christians to seek peace and to focus their lives on the salvation of their souls. The other view, that drawn by Titian, proposes the ordering of the Christian world according to the prescriptions of the Church whose head, the Pope, is ruler of the Res Publica Christiana. These opposing views about the nature and function of the Church are almost as old as the Church itself. Sometimes the differences were muted; at other times they came out into the open, leading to conflict and clashes.

The War of the League of Cambrai offered a striking example of a disturbing fusion of spiritual and secular interests. These interests were mixed in almost all the issues and conflicts discussed in this book—the price of alum, the salt monopoly, loan guarantees, navigation rights, territorial claims, juridical disputes. There had always been some doubt about this intermingling of spiritual and secular interests, and the study of the world of Greece and Rome and closer acquaintance with ancient philosophy served to increase the questioning. It is no accident, however, that criticism mounted to a high pitch in the time of Julius II. He showed less hesitation to use both spiritual and secular weapons than any other pope before him.

Julius had grasped for the papal crown as if it belonged to him, and he identified himself with all the rights the papacy possessed and claimed. But in his case the medieval claim that the head of the Church has supreme power in spiritual and secular affairs received impetus from the belief in the strength of human will and human powers which the revival of interest in antiquity had fostered.

The role Julius assigned to the papacy demanded that the pope be fully independent. The papal states must be made equal to if not stronger than the other Italian states. The influence of foreign powers on Italian affairs had to be limited, and the ultimate aim was pursued with boundless energy: to drive the barbarians from Italy. Julius brought into the Italian politics of his time an ingredient of national feeling, an appeal to Italian national pride. The individual issues, which Julius negotiated and for which he went to war, were often minor, and in his demands he could show a petty obstinacy; but his goals were based on principles he was not willing to compromise. In triumph and in defeat he was an awesome figure, the "papa terribile"; behind his policy was passion and a great concept.

114

Still, an unavoidable consequence of the policy Julius pursued was that it magnified the obstacles on the road to his goals, thus preventing their attainment. The indiscriminate use of spiritual and secular weapons—as natural as it might have appeared to Julius—raised doubted about the authority of the papacy. Erasmus, both in *Julius Exclusus* and *Praise of Folly*, ridiculing the "thunderbolt of excommunication,"[8] of "the papal bull which by a flicker hurls the souls of men to the depths of hell,"[9] again stakes out the most radical position by entirely denying the efficacy of papal censures. But for most—individuals and governments—excommunication continued to remain a serious concern. And because of Julius' application of spiritual weapons in political contests, his enemies also felt entitled to use spiritual weapons. The remark Priuli made in his diary,[10] when he had heard of the convocation of a council by Louis XII and then of a counter-council by Julius II, is characteristic of the decline of ecclesiastical authority: the political motive in the convocation of these two councils seemed to him so obvious that neither could be a free, true council. The employment of the Pope's spiritual powers in the service of political purposes fatally weakened the Pope's claim to be mediator and judge in conflicts among the European rulers.

Moreover, involvement in secular politics made the Pope a partisan: he had to seek the support of other princes, and by allying himself with one group of European states, he aroused the hostility of others. Thus papal policy played its part in widening the rifts among the European powers and strengthened the trend toward the development of a system of sovereign states. The Pope himself contributed to the breakup of the Res Publica Christiana. The War of the League of Cambrai has a Janus face. In its declared aims and ideological justifications it went back to the concepts of the past, but it was also fought with the modern instruments of power—diplomacy, finances, soldiers—and became a struggle for a balance of power in a system of sovereign states.

Erasmus' hope that the Pope, by abandoning all worldly splendor and power, would be able to fulfill his function as a peacemaker and Titian's vision of the Church as the actual ruler of the world reflect that dual aspects of Julius' policy and proclaimed the need to overcome these contradictions. The concepts of Erasmus and Titian were too extreme to be realized. With Julius II's failure to drive the barbarians out of Italy, the possibility of establishing the papacy as arbiter in European politics disappeared. With the major European powers marching into Italy, Italy could no longer determine its own fate. New protagonists came forward with new aims, and gradually the center of gravity shifted to new arenas. This also eliminated any prospect for creating a golden age of peace, as Erasmus and many others had expected of Julius' successor, Leo X.[11] The Pope could not risk a challenge to the existence of foreign rule on Italian soil. He was content with trying to secure for himself a certain amount of freedom of action by playing one foreign power against another. The mines of Tolfa remained profitable, but there was no longer the possibility of a European alum monopoly.[12] Court bankers continued to strive to become as rich and powerful as Chigi, but the papal state was now too small a base for their operations and they looked to the courts of Europe's powerful secular rulers.

Only Venice emerged from the War of the League of Cambrai in roughly the same position it had at the beginning of the war: it had regained its former territories.[13] Although the Venetians tried to give the impression that they remained a great European power, their actions show that they knew they could no longer chart their own course. In the struggles between France and Spain, their moves were directed toward one goal: to be on the side of the stronger power. Venice began to live on its ability to engage in a balancing act rather than on its own strength. In order to close the gap between the outward splendor of the city and the diminishing influence Venice exerted on European politics, the Venetians turned to the past and began to live on the images of their former greatness.[14] The dream that they were still

116

a great power was kept alive by the paintings in the council halls of the ducal palace. But in considering the world around them, the Venetian nobles, walking from the Senate to the Collegio, probably felt an admonition to cautiousness rather than an appeal to action when they gazed at Palma's painting celebrating the victory of Venice over the League of Cambrai.

NOTES

INDEX

ABBREVIATIONS

ASF	Archivio di Stato, Firenze
ASR	Archivio di Stato, Roma
ASS	Archivio di Stato, Siena
ASV	Archivio di Stato, Venezia
A.Vat.	*Archivio Secreto Vaticano*
Bibl. Correr, *Priuli*	Priuili, *I Diarii*, unpublished manuscript in Biblioteca Correr
BV, Arch. Chigi	Biblioteca Vaticana, Archivio Chigi
Cugnoni	Cugnoni's biography of Chigi
DBI	*Dizionario biografico italiano*
Gritti	*Provveditor general in terra firma, Gritti 1510*
Sanudo	*I Diarii di Marino Sanuto*

Notes

I. Venice in the War of the League of Cambrai

1. Francesco Sansovino, *Venetia città nobilissima e singolare*, ed. D. Giustinian Martinioni (Venice, 1663), p. 344. The description I quote is one of Martinioni's additions; the original edition was published in 1581. Palma's painting is also discussed in Staale Sinding-Larsen, *Christ in the Council Hall* (Rome, 1974), pp. 40, 247.

2. Heinrich Kretschmayr, *Geschichte von Venedig*, II (Gotha, 1920), chap. 17, provides a full story of the war from the Venetian point of view. For papal policy, see Ludwig Pastor, *History of the Popes*, VI (London, 1898), book 2, chaps. 4 and 5, and Moritz Brosch, *Papst Julius II und die Gruendung des Kirchenstaates* (Gotha, 1878), chaps. 5 and 6. For a description of the military operations in 1510-11, see Piero Pieri, *Il Rinascimento e la crisi militare italiana* (Turin, 1952), pp. 478-483. For the impact of the battle of Agnadello, see also Innocento Cervelli, *Machiavelli e la crisi dello stato veneziano* (Naples, 1974), esp. chap. 8.

3. Venetian institutions have been treated in a large number of writings, which do not always agree because they focus on different periods. If my outline differs in some details from what can be found elsewhere, the reason is that I am concerned with the situation in 1511 and make extensive use of what I learned about the functioning of the institutions in archival research. Of course, I have also made use of the scholarly literature. The standard work is Giuseppe Maranini, *La Costituzione di Venezia* (Perugia, 1931). See also the short outlines of the constitution in James C. Davis, *The Decline of the Venetian Nobility as a Ruling Class* (Baltimore, 1962), chap. 1; D. S. Chambers, *The Imperial Age of Venice* (London, 1970), pp. 73-80, and Sinding-Larsen, *Christ in the Council Hall*, pp. 120-155. Also Frederic C. Lane, *Venice: A Maritime Republic* (Baltimore, 1973), p. 429, fig. 40.

4. *I Diarii di Marino Sanuto* (Venice, 1879-1903), 58 vols.; hence-

forth cited *Sanudo* ("Sanudo," the Venetian form of "Sanuto," is generally used in the literature).

5. Girolamo Priuli, *I Diarii*, ed. R. Cessi (Rerum Italicarum Scriptores, XXIV, part 3, Bologna, 1933-1937); the later parts of this diary, which contain the material important for the present study, are still unpublished. They can be found in Biblioteca Correr, Provenienze Diverse, 252, esp. vol. VI; henceforth cited Bibl. Correr, *Priuli*.

6. Estimates of the size of the Venetian population in the sixteenth century are very rough; more exact figures are available only from the end of the sixteenth century on, and the book by Daniele Beltrami, *Storia della popolazione di Venezia dalla fine del secolo XVI alla caduta della republica* (Padova, 1954), concentrates on the more recent centuries. Karl Julius Beloch, *Bevoelkerungsgeschichte Italiens*, III (Berlin, 1961), deals in his chapter on "Die Republik Venedig" with earlier times, and his conclusion is that Venice at the time of the beginning of the War of the League of Cambrai had something like 102,000 inhabitants. Refer to Davis, *Decline*, p. 55, for a careful consideration of the various estimates.

7. F. Lane has shown, in "The Enlargement of the Great Council of Venice," *Florilegium Historiale*, ed. J. G. Rowe and W. H. Stockdale (Toronto, 1971), pp. 236-274, that the traditional term "closing" is a misnomer.

8. For a detailed study of the development, composition, and functions of the Senate, see Enrico Besta, *Il Senato veneziano* (Miscellanea di Storia Veneta, ser. 2, vol. V; Venice, 1899).

9. The best analysis of this office, particularly in the first centuries of its existence, is Reinhold C. Mueller, "The Procurators of San Marco in the Thirteenth and Fourteenth Centuries: A Study of the Office as a Financial and Trust Institution," *Studi veneziani*, XIII (1971), 105-220.

10. According to Z. S. Fink, *The Classical Republicans* (2nd ed., Evanston, 1962), the simile of the pyramid for Venice was "a Renaissance commonplace." On the development of the notion of Venice as realization of an ideal government, see my chapter, "The Venetian Constitution in Florentine Political Thought," in *History: Choice and Commitment* (Cambridge, Mass., 1977), esp. pp. 182-187. Contarini's *De magistratibus et republica venetorum*, of course, was the most famous and most influential work idealizing Venice; on the date of its composition, see my "The Date of the Composition of Contarini's and Gian-

notti's Books on Venice," *Studies in the Renaissance*, XIV (1967), 176-177.

11. The Civico Museo Correr on the Piazza San Marco contains a large collection of official robes; this exhibition and paintings show the differences much more clearly than the rather sketchy descriptions in books.

II. Chigi in Venice

1. Sanudo's entries about Chigi's arrival in Venice and about the banquet given by Grimani in his honor will be found in *Sanudo*, XI, cols. 794, 834-835, 841.

2. For Chigi's relations with the Spannocchi and with Alexander VI and Julius II, see Chapter III of this book.

3. The Cappelli of Santa Maria Materdomini—one branch of this very large "clan"—undertook various banking enterprises. In the 1480s, three brothers—Andrea, Alvise, and Paolo, the provveditore of 1510-11—opened a bank together with Tommaso Lippomani; in 1507 the brothers Antonio, Silvano, and Vettore opened a bank together with the Vendramin, and this bank was very active during the War of the League of Cambrai. Piero Cappello, who together with his brother Lorenzo, is mentioned as guest at the Grimani party, was married to a Vendramin. See the articles about these members of the Cappelli family in *Dizionario biografico italiano* (henceforth cited *DBI*).

4. For the following, see Archivio di Stato, Venezia (henceforth abbreviated ASV), *Senato terra*, reg. 16, f.146r, and reg. 17, f.30v. For the settling of the Jews in Venice, see Brian Pullan, *Rich and Poor in Renaissance Venice* (Oxford, 1971), pp. 478-481.

5. ASV, *Senato mar*, reg. 17, February 10, 1511, et seq.; *Dieci misto*, reg. 33, June 20, 1510; also *Sanudo*, XI, col. 146. For an explanation of the Venetian convoy system, see Frederic C. Lane, "Fleets and Fairs," in his collected papers, *Venice and History* (Baltimore, 1966), pp. 128-141.

6. A list of goods carried by a convoy to Alexandria can be found in *Sanudo*, XII, cols. 77-78.

7. See ASV, *Senato mar*, reg. 17, January 28, 1510. Gino Luzzatto, *Storia economica di Venezia dall' XI al XVI secolo* (Venice, 1961), p. 248, tells of the measures taken to prevent starvation but also states that

the buying of great amounts of grain was not necessary. For statistics about the amount of grain imported into Venice in 1511 and 1512, see *Sanudo*, XV, col. 146.

8. The relevant documents are published in Henry Simonsfeld, *Der Fondaco dei Tedeschi in Venedig* (Stuttgart, 1887), I, 377ff; also see II, 120-133.

9. See *Sanudo*, XI, col. 720.

10. Suspension of salary payments during the War of Cambrai was first ordered in a decree by the Pregadi dated April 19, 1509; the full text can be found in *Sanudo*, VIII, cols. 101-103; the decree was adopted by the Great Council on April 22.

11. ASV, *Senato mar*, reg. 27, February 27, 1512.

12. See letters of the Venetian merchant Martino Merlini, published in G. Dalla Santa, "Commerci, vita privata e notizie politiche dei giorni della Lega di Cambrai," *Atti del Reale Istituto Veneto di Scienze, Lettere ed Arti*, LXXVI, part 2 (1916-1917); p. 1559 on doubling of the prices for grain.

13. Dalla Santa, p. 1559: "Non se vede ni se raxona d'altro cha di guera, morbo e charestia, ma la guera pasa el tuto, fa desmentegar el morbo, perchè l'e venuto quel tenpo che dixeva nostri antezesori, ch'el vegnerà ch'el vivo averà invidia al morto."

14. Dalla Santa, p. 1558: "fazo pivi dela mita de la setemana senza charne, e del vin te so dir ch'el batizo in la barila." For the references to Merlini's letters, see ibid., pp. 1549-1553, 1554-1566; on Merlini's plans to settle in the country, pp. 1572-1573; the story of the parrot is on p. 1576.

15. For the increase of taxes during the war years, see the list of taxes imposed between 1500 and 1515 published in *Sanudo*, XX, cols. 7-15.

16. See Dalla Santa, pp. 1563, 1572.

17. *Sanudo*, XI, col. 733.

18. *Sanudo*, XI, col. 794.

19. ASV, *Senato terra*, reg. 17, February 14, 1511, and the brief report in *Sanudo*, XI, cols. 815-816.

20. The decree is published in *Sanudo*, XI, cols. 796-799 (with a wrong date of February 4 instead of February 15).

21. *Sanudo*, XI, col. 841.

22. Alvise Pisani was Savio della Terra Firma from November 1508 to March 1509, and from January to June in 1510, 1511, 1512, and 1513;

Lorenzo Cappello was Savio della Terra Firma, January to June 1511, April to September 1512, January to June 1513; Piero Cappello was Savio Grande, July to December 1509, April to September 1510. Legally it was not permitted to be "uninterruptedly" a member of the Savi since, after your term was over, you had to wait till you could be reelected for as many months as you had held office. In the cases of Alvise Pisani and Lorenzo and Piero Cappello, this rule was kept. However, it was possible to circumvent the rule in wartime by serving as a kind of adjunct Savio immediately after your term had ended. This issue, and the friction it caused, is discussed on pp. 45-49.

23. For the following, see the summary in *Sanudo*, VII, cols. 689-691, 697 and 705-709; the detailed figures given in cols. 705-709 correspond to the document in ASV, *Senato terra*, December 23, 1508. *Sanudo*, VII, col. 690, indicates that the war budget amounted to 249,000 ducats; by using the same figures, I arrive at a somewhat lower sum of 235,000 ducats, but for present purposes this difference is of no significance.

24. See *Sanudo*, VII, col. 690, which explains why the figure on col. 706 is slightly different.

25. The composition of the Venetian army at the start of the campaign in April 1509 is described in *Sanudo*, VIII, cols. 149-152. Sanudo's figures are slightly lower than those given by Piero Pieri, *Il Rinascimento*, p. 458. According to Pieri, the Venetian army at the beginning of hostilities amounted to 10,000 horsemen and 20,000 foot soldiers.

26. The most detailed and most authoritative statement about the Venetian tax system and the origin of its various taxes will be found in the publication of the Reale Commissione per la Pubblicazione dei Documenti Finanziari della Repubblica di Venezia: *Serie seconda, Bilanci generali*, I (Venice, 1912). The decima is discussed in the introduction on pp. cxlviii-cliii, and the various monti on pp. cxci-cxcii. On p. clvii, see also the discussion of the *tansa*, a tax added to the decima; it was estimated on the basis of a person's or family's entire property and could amount to a "loan" of 300 ducats. It was frequently raised during the War of the League of Cambrai, but aroused heavy opposition. For a concise and clear survey of the financial policy of the Venetian Republic, see Gino Luzzatto, *Storia economica di Venezia dal XI al XVI secolo* (Venice, 1961), pp. 207-213, 238-239. Luzzatto in *Storia*

economica, pp. 211-212, and Lane in *Venice*, p. 237, make attempts to reconstruct the budget of the Venetian Republic; these reconstructions are based on *Bilanci generali*, pp. 171-173. The great difference between Luzzatto and Lane can be explained by Lane's inclusion of income from the terra firma and from overseas possessions. I find it difficult to believe that before 1509 the Venetians had an annual surplus of 620,000 ducats available for extraordinary expenses (war). I suspect that, in these reconstructed budgets, the income figures are too high and the expense figures too low.

A ducat contained 3.55 grams of pure gold. A noble who had an annual income of less than 1000 ducats was considered to be badly off. On the other hand, there was an immense difference between the incomes of nobles and laborers. An unskilled laborer earned 15-20 ducats annually; a skilled craftsman could make only 50 ducats in one year. See Lane, *Venice*, p. 333.

27. On the imposition of taxes in 1500-1515, see *Sanudo*, XX, cols. 7-15; although Sanudo's statistics are not reliable, the relationship between the years before 1509 and the years after 1509 is certainly correct. In general, on the attempt to increase the tax revenues see my "Venice in the Crisis of the League of Cambrai," in *History: Choice and Commitment*, pp. 269-291.

28. For the first important measures regarding the sale of offices, see *Sanudo*, X, cols. 37-39, 44, and for the names of the people who entered the Pregadi on the basis of payments, see ASV, *Dieci misto*, reg. 33, last page; for the lowering of the price of entry, see ibid., September 4, 1510, f.132v.

29. The quotations from reports of Gritti and Cappello come from ASV, *Provveditor general in terra firma, Gritti 1510*, vol. 27, 28 (henceforth cited as *Gritti*). Although the volume is called *Gritti*, it also contains reports from Cappello from the time when the army was united and Cappello and Gritti were together; but after the army was divided, the volume is limited to Gritti's reports. Cappello's reports are not preserved, although we can draw some conclusions about their contents from files such as *Dieci misto* and from Sanudo's *Diarii*.

30. *Sanudo*, XI, col. 561.

31. *Gritti*, vol. 28, f.59r, October 29, 1510.

32. *Gritti*, vol. 28, f.115, November 27, 1510.

33. *Gritti,* vol. 28, f.143v, December 9, 1510.

34. *Gritti,* vol. 28, f.208, January 15, 1511.

35. *Gritti,* vol. 28, f.159ff, December 14, 1510.

36. From the end of January on, Gritti expressed concern that the troops might desert if they received no regular payments; the most detailed report about the threat of the condottieri to mutiny is in *Gritti,* vol. 29, dated April 2, 1511. *Sanudo,* XII, col. 72, noted that similar reports about refusal of the soldiers to fight arrived from Cappello.

37. See Bibl. Correr, *Priuli,* VI, f.123v-124r.

38. *Priuli,* f.109r.

39. *Priuli,* f.111r-112r. I give a somewhat abbreviated resume of Priuli's long and repetitive discussion.

40. For the payments of Cappello in March, see ASV, *Dieci misto,* reg. 34, March 19 and March 27, 1511; these decrees also state the securities that the bankers received for their loans. Since Cappello's reports are not preserved, we have no way of knowing whether he also received money from other sources; it seems unlikely. Gritti, according to ASV, *Dieci misto,* January 3, f.174r, was to receive 3000 ducats from the Pisani bank and from Cappello-Vendramin; in a report dated January 13 (*Gritti,* f.205v), he stated that he had been able to pay the "Gente d'arme" but not the "governatore." All his further reports emphasize his urgent financial needs. Early in March, f.323r, Gritti gives a kind of accounting of the money he has received in January and February—it amounts to 8627 ducats. It has to be admitted that the documentation indicating the sums sent to the provveditori is not complete, and we have to use different sources that are not in complete accord. On one hand we have the decrees of the Council of Ten which inform us when loans were received and about the securities these loans required: these transactions had to be approved by the Council. On the other hand, we have Gritti's reports: a cautious estimate based on these sources (and "cautious" means too high rather than too low) allows us to conclude that the monthly payments to the armies in the field in the first months of 1511 amounted to 25,000 ducats. Finally, the Pisani bank gave advances to the government in other areas too.

Professor John R. Hale was kind enough to allow me to read the manuscript of his work on "Venice, the Military Organization of a Renaissance State, 1509-1617"; he provides estimates of the monthly payroll.

Because of the unevenness of the sources, these estimates, as Hale states, are very rough and only approximate. According to Hale, the payroll expenses for 1511 were 538,400 ducats; this sum includes the entire Venetian military force, not only the armies fighting in northern Italy against France. It must also be noted that the amounts needed in the first four months of 1511 were lower than those in the summer months and in the rest of the year because in July and August the army was enlarged from 11,000 to 16,000 men. It might be concluded that, at the time when the negotiations with Chigi were taking place, the monthly expenses for the troops fighting against the French amounted to 25-30,000 ducats. 40,000 ducats would defray expenses for six weeks to two months. During this period no new taxes would have to be imposed; nor would the Venetian patricians be required to grant forced loans. The hard-pressed bankers would have the possibility to receive from the securities which had been given to them some repayment of their advances. This explains the attraction that Chigi's offer had for the Venetian rulers and the statements of men like Girolamo Priuli who believed that the continued existence of Venice depended on the conclusion of the contract. On the other hand, it is also an example of the hand-to-mouth war financing that characterizes the entire period.

41. Rumors about a peace at the expense of Venice were widespread. See, for instance, the report of the Florentine ambassador at the French headquarters in Milan of March 21, 1511, who had heard from the Spanish ambassador at the Curia that there were no real conflicts among the King of France, Maximilian, and the Pope and that the only difficulties were the hostility of the Pope against the Duke of Ferrara and the conflicts between Maximilian and Venice; but the King of France ought to be able to persuade the Duke of Ferrara to give in, and the Pope would be able to force Venice to make concessions—Archivio di Stato, Firenze (henceforth abbreviated ASF), *Signori, X di balia, VIII di pratica: Legazioni e commissarie: Missive e responsive*, reg. 70, f.146v. Actually Julius II probably was not willing to make peace with France, but an agreement between Matthaeus Lang, the Bishop of Gurk and Maximilian's negotiator, and the Pope was widely expected: Venice would retain on the terra firma only Padova and Treviso and would pay Maximilian a tribute (report in the same volume of April 17, 1511, f.157).

III. The Contract

1. *Sanudo*, XII, col. 14.

2. For details about the monopoly of the Tolfa alum mines in Christian Europe and Chigi's role as "farmer" of the mines, see the next chapter.

3. *Sanudo*, XII, col. 77.

4. Detailed contemporary descriptions of the earthquake will be found in *Sanudo*, XII, cols. 79-84 and 87, and Bibl. Correr, *Priuli*, VI, ff.129r-131v.

5. On Giustiniani and Quirino and their circle, to which Gasparo Contarini, later reforming Cardinal, belonged, see my "Religion and Politics in the Thought of Gasparo Contarini," in *History: Choice and Commitment*, pp. 247-267. Giustiniani left Venice for Camaldoli in December 1510; Quirino followed ten months later.

6. See ASV, *Dieci misto*, reg. 34, March 27, 1511, ff.64v-65r, for the decree against homosexuality, and *Sanudo*, XII, cols. 98-99, 110-111, for the measures on the Jews.

7. *Sanudo*, XII, col. 85.

8. *Sanudo*, XII, col. 117.

9. Bibl. Correr, *Priuli*, VI, ff.153v-156r, discusses the arguments advanced for and against the arrangement with Chigi in the debates of the councils and the Pregadi. Priuli did not like the arrangement, but he believed the contract ought to be concluded. My description is based on Priuli, along with the quotations.

10. Grimani and Corner were leading papalisti—that is, Venetian nobles who, having close relations with people serving at the Curia, had to leave the Great Council when relations with the Pope were under discussion. A list of papalisti at the beginning of 1509 will be found in *Sanudo*, VII, cols. 734-735, which contains many names we later find among the advocates of the contract with Chigi: Piero Diedo, Batista Boldù, Bernardo Bembo, Niccolò Michiel, Zacaria Gabriel, Antonio Cappello, and so on.

11. The dates about membership in the Council of Savi are derived from the files of the Senato Terra.

12. See *Sanudo*, III, esp. col. 389; at that time, Antonio Tron was a leader in the Venetian ruling group.

13. On Grimani's solemn return from exile, see *Sanudo*, VIII, col. 555, also 411.

14. For clashes in the Pregadi between Grimani and Tron, with Tron being regularly outvoted, see *Sanudo*, IX, cols. 242, 275, 281/2, 344, 441; *X*, cols. 8, 25. For the Grimani-Tron relation, see also Robert Finlay, "Venice, the Po Expedition, and the End of the League of Cambrai, 1509-1510," *Studies in Modern European History and Culture*, II (1976), 37-72; Finlay considers Grimani as leader of a war party, Tron as a moderate.

15. *Sanudo*, VIII, col. 254.

16. *Sanudo*, VIII, col. 284.

17. See *Sanudo*, IX, col. 461.

18. ASV, *Sento terra*, reg. 16, f.133v.

19. Grimani and Corner were regular Savi Grandi; Domenico Trevisan was an·adjunct member; Tron and Corner were from the same group of Procurators. It is clear that a change of the law was necessary if all three—Grimani, Corner, Trevisan—or at least two of them were to remain in the Council of Savi.

20. See ASV, *Senato terra*, reg. 17, July 11, 1511, f.80v; *Sanudo*, XII, cols. 283, 287.

21. *Sanudo*, XII, col. 288: "Fe' mal, judifio meo."

22. For the proposal of Tron and Delfin, see ASV, *Senato terra*, reg. 17, September 12, 1511, f.105v; Delfin's opposition to the Grimani group appears from his interventions in the Pregadi—see *Sanudo*, index. In May 1511, Delfin was the one Savio who did not support the contract with Chigi; see ASV, *Senato secreta*, reg. 44, May 15, 1511.

23. *Sanudo*, XII, col. 136.

24. *Sanudo*, XII, col. 139.

25. *Sanudo*, XII, col. 163.

26. For a short report, see *Sanudo*, XII, col. 164; for details, see ASV, *Senato secreta*, reg. 44, May 7, 1511. It may be remarked that the names of the three negotiators given by Sanudo are not identical with those given in *Senato secreta* (Domenico Trevisan and Alvise Mocenigo instead of Giorgio Corner and Pietro Lando). According to *Senato secreta* the election took place only on May 8; Sanudo may have given the names of people who were elected on May 7 but then rejected; *Senato secreta* gives only the final results.

27. See *Sanudo*, XII, col. 173.

28. ASV, *Senato secreta*, reg. 44, May 12, 1511; *Sanudo*, XII, col. 174.

29. ASV, *Senato secreta*, reg. 44, May 15, 1511; *Sanudo*, XII, col. 179.

30. See ASV, *Senato secreta*, reg. 44, particularly under May 12, 1511, the memorandum describing the various issues. But for an understanding of the arrangements the long discussion in Bibl. Correr, *Priuli*, VI, ff. 196r-197v, is valuable and has been used in my analysis of the contracts. Copies of the legal documents are in the ASV, *Libri commemoriali*, XIX, nos. 196 and 197.

31. The name used in the documents for the measure is *miara* (thousandweight), but since later on, for the same amount of alum, the much better-known term *cantaro* is used, I apply this term here. The weight of one cantaro differs in various parts of Italy but is somewhat below 50 kilograms (47 kilograms in most parts of northern Italy). The ducats are specifically designated as *ducati d'oro*, as might be expected—7000 cantari amounted to 25 percent of the annual production of alum in Tolfa. See Jean Delumeau, *L'Alun de Rome XV-XIX siècle* (École Pratique des Hautes Études—VI section, Centre de Recherches Historiques: Ports, routes, trafics, XIII; Paris, 1962), p. 134.

32. *Sanudo*, XII, col. 187.

33. Bibl. Correr, *Priuli*, VI, f.324v, written in August.

34. ASV, *Senato secreta*, reg. 44, May 17, 1511.

35. The events described in my text are discussed at length in Pastor, *History of the Popes*, and in Brosch, *Papst Julius II*. Francesco Guicciardini, in his *Storia d'Italia*, book IX, gives probably the most penetrating analysis of the attitude of Julius II in this crisis; the epitaph on the death of the Cardinal of Bologna comes from book IX, chap. 18.

36. ASV, *Senato secreta*, reg. 44, to "Oratori in Curia," June 16, 1511. Also Bibl. Correr, *Priuli*, VI, f.277v.

37. Ibid., f.246r.

38. Ibid., f.271v.

39. Ibid., f.259r.

40. Ibid., f.313r.

41. ASV, *Senato secreta*, reg. 44, to "Oratori in Curia," July 14 and 15, 1511, indicates what the ambassador reported about the Pope's negotiations; the reports of the Venetian ambassador from the Curia are not preserved.

42. *Sanudo*, XII, cols. 299, 327. According to Guicciardini, book IX, chap. 18, immediately after the fall of Bologna, Julius II asked for the return of the money sent for the Swiss to Venice some time earlier, but this had not been done; it was significant, therefore, that the Pope now decided that the money should be used as originally intended. See Bibl. Correr, *Priuli*, VI, f.205v, for the transfer of 5000 ducats to Pisani, 5000 ducats to Cappello-Vendramin, and 10,000 ducats to Chigi from Rome to Venice for the Swiss.

43. *Sanudo*, XX, cols. 314-318, indicates some of the payments that were made to the troops during spring and summer—in small, delayed installments.

44. Bibl. Correr, *Priuli*, VI, f.326v, written in August 1511.

45. Ibid., f.306v, written in July 1511. This page, and the preceding ff.304v-305r, give a graphic description of the Venetian despair over the financial and military situation.

46. Ibid., f.261r, v. This is a long discussion on the decline of Venetian morals, written in June 1511.

47. *Sanudo*, XII, cols. 277-278.

48. Johannes Wilde, *Venetian Art from Bellini to Titian* (Oxford, 1974), esp. chaps. 3 and 4.

49. One reads in histories of art that Titian went to Padua because living there was more secure than in besieged Venice, but this is a complete misunderstanding. If life was unsafe, it was in Padua in 1511.

50. Bibl. Correr, *Priuli*, VI, f.306v; see also *Sanudo*, XII, col. 336. He was one of the people who gave Chigi pledges as security for the loan.

51. See ASV, *Dieci misto*, reg. 34, July 16, 17, 26, 29, September 15; also *Sanudo*, XII, col. 291.

52. Strangely enough, there is no documentary material on the Franza affair in the Venetian archives, at least not after he had been brought back from Cattaro to Venice (the letters to the governor of Cattaro demanding Franza's return to Venice, printed *Sanudo*, XII, cols. 151-153, are in the archives). My account therefore is based on *Sanudo*, XI, cols. 814, 834, 835; XII, cols. 120, 168, 280, 286, 287, 289, 300, 305, 320; XVI, col. 524.

53. In Biblioteca Vaticana, *Archivio Chigi*, arm. 290, no. 11451, is an agreement between Franza and Chigi, dated August 28, 1513, which

is concerned with a cloth deal valued at 4000 ducats. It looks to me as if this might be concealed repayment of Franza's debt and perhaps a prerequisite of his release from prison, but this is pure speculation. (The abbreviation "arm." is for Armadio, the large cupboard in which documents are kept in the Vatican.)

54. The relevant documents can be found in ASV, *Libri commemoriali*, XIX, nos. 197, 201-204, 238. Perhaps it ought to be mentioned here that on May 21, 1511, immediately after the approval of the basic contract with Chigi, the Venetian government prohibited the import of any alum, which did not fall under the contract with Chigi; ASV, *Dieci misto*, reg. 34, May 21, 1511.

55. Bibl. Correr, *Priuli*, VI, f.334r.

56. For instance, ibid., f.26r.

57. Ibid., f.343r. Although Priuli declared several times that he had difficulties in explaining the contract with Chigi, actually his discussion of the arrangement and of the changes between the contract planned in May and the final arrangements of August is very enlightening; see ibid., ff.324r, 325r, v, 342v-344r.

58. *Sanudo*, XII, col. 324; the two Trons who assailed the contract were Sante Tron and Luca Tron, Antonio's son.

59. See Bibl. Correr, *Priuli*, VI, f.333v; Sanudo, XII, col. 336.

60. The complete list of the fifty is in ASV, *Libri commemoriali*, XIX, no. 201.

61. In these business transactions, Besalù acted as Chigi's representative; see, for instance, ASV, *Dieci misto*, reg. 34, August 14, 1511. Also *Sanudo*, XII, col. 376.

62. *Sanudo*, XII, col. 342.

63. Sanudo reports the departure in the same detail with which he had reported Chigi's arrival; XII, cols. 378, 393.

IV. Chigi in Rome

1. Fabio Chigi's biography was published by Giuseppe Cugnoni, in *Archivio della R. Società Romana di Storia Patria*, II (1879), 46-83. Cugnoni added an introduction and extended commentaries that contain valuable material from the Chigi archives and from public archives; see *Archivio della R. Società Romana*, II, 37-45, 209-226, 475-490; III

(1880), 213-232, 291-305, 422-448; IV (1881), 56-75, 195-216; VI (1883), 139-172, 497-539. This material, used extensively, is henceforth cited *Cugnoni*.

2. See, for instance, Melissa M. Bullard, "Mercatores florentini romanam curiam sequentes," *Journal of Medieval and Renaissance Studies*, VI (1976), 51-71.

3. See the important article by Clemens Bauer, "Studi per la storia delle finanze papali durante il pontificato di Sisto IV," *Archivio della R. Società Romana*, L (1927), 319-400; although concerned with a somewhat earlier period, A. Gottlob, *Aus der Camera Apostolica des 15. Jahrhunderts* (Innsbruck, 1889), gives a valuable outline of the entire financial system of the Curia. The two volumes by Walther von Hofmann, *Forschungen zur Geschichte der kurialen Behoerden vom Schisma bis zur Reformation* (Rome, 1914), have little bearing on the questions with which we are concerned. Jean Delumeau, *Vie économique et sociale de Rome dans la seconde moitié du XVI siècle* (BEFAR, CLXXXIV; Paris, 1959), deals with a later situation, in which the financial administration of the papal states used different means, namely the monti, instead of tax farming. Nevertheless, chapter 2 of part III, "Difficultés financières de la papauté," is important because of its outline of the general situation and its discussion of the fragmentary character of the source material; this explains why the subject of papal finances is so difficult to treat with precision.

4. Next to Bauer, "Studi," pp. 325ff, see Aloys Schulte, *Die Fugger in Rom*, I (Leipzig, 1904), esp. chaps. 2 and 3.

5. That part of the papal income with which the Italian bankers were particularly concerned, the revenues from the papal states, from the fifteenth century on played a decisive role in the budget. See Wolfgang Reinhardt, *Papstfinanz und Nepotismus unter Paul V (1605-1621)*, (Paepste und Papsttum, VI, part 1; Stuttgart, 1974), p. 1, and Peter Partner, "The Budget of the Roman Church," *Italian Renaissance Studies*, ed. E. F. Jacob (London, 1960), pp. 256-278.

6. For a recent general statement about the practice of tax farming, see *The Cambridge Economic History of Europe*, III (Cambridge, 1963), pp. 437-438. For an example of an advance given by tax farmers, and the repayment of this advance by means of deductions from the annual payments that the tax farmers had to make to the Curia, see Partner, "The Budget," p. 276, entry on fo.597.

7. In chapter 10 of the first part of Burckhardt's *Civilization of the Renaissance in Italy*.

8. Julius II and Leo X exempted the rulers of Naples from paying, beyond sending a horse as tribute; see Moroni's *Dizionario storico-ecclesiastico*, XIII, "Chinea." It ought to be said that, under Clemens VII in 1525, a census of 7000 ducats from Naples is listed; see Partner, "The Budget," p. 275. For the tribute paid by Ferrara and Urbino, I have used the figures given by Bauer, "Finanze papali," p. 389-390; Partner's figures are slightly different, but the budget that Bauer published, pp. 349-392, is more detailed and slightly closer in time to the period with which we are dealing. However, differences in the figures are quite unavoidable because they were estimates rather than based on receipts. The difficulties in arriving at precise figures can be clearly seen in Partner, "The Budget," pp. 270-273. Before 1530, only a very few, chronologically widely separated budget estimates were preserved (or were attempted); they have been analyzed with great care in the above-mentioned writings of Bauer, Gottlob, and Partner. I shall rely on these writings and add some material from documents I studied in the Vatican Archives.

9. For a short characterization of the various Roman taxes, see Bauer, "Finanze papali," p. 338.

10. This Dogana delle Merce was also called Dogana di S. Eustachio because the office was near the Church of San Eustachio. According to Augustin Theiner, *Codex diplomaticus dominii temporalis santae sedis* (Rome, 1862), III, f.506, it was farmed out under Innocent VIII for 8000 ducats.

11. Dogana di Ripa.

12. Dogana delle Grascie or Grascia.

13. For the Gabella Studii see D. S. Chambers, "Studium Urbis and Gabella Studii: The University of Rome in the Fifteenth Century," *Cultural Aspects of the Italian Renaissance*, ed. C. Clough (Manchester, 1976), pp. 68-110.

14. Dogana delle Pecore or dei Pascoli. An interesting discussion of this tax will be found in A. Anzilotto, "Cenni sulle finanze del patrimonio di San Pietro," *Archivio della R. Società Romana*, XLII (1919), 365-375.

15. The title was Depositorio Generale.

16. For instance, see *Archivio Secreto Vaticano* (henceforth abbreviated A.Vat.), arm. XXXIV, vol. 13, f.94r ff, about the wine tax of Bo-

logna given to the brothers Casali of that town.

17. We have figures about the income from the salt tax in the two "budgets" from the time of Pope Sixtus IV, the one published by Gottlob, *Camera apostolica*, pp. 253-255, the other (securely dated 1480-81) by Bauer, "Finanze papali," pp. 349-392. There are also figures in an interesting document—a report of the outgoing Cardinal treasurer, Cardinal Francesco Borgia to his successor Hadrian de Castello, dated October 28, 1500, A.Vat., arm. XXXIV, vol. 11, f.333r-336v (Peter Partner was kind enough to give me a copy he had made). The figures in these three sources are not identical since they come from various years. For us it is important that they agree in the relationship of values among the various taxes. I shall indicate the value that these three sources assign to the various taxes; G. will indicate the figure in the document published by Gottlob, B. that in Bauer's document, and V. that in the document from the Vatican Archives. It ought to be remarked that Partner has published a budget from 1525 in his "The Budget," pp. 275-278, but this document deals with the various taxes so summarily that it cannot be used for comparative purposes; the figures for the most profitable of the taxes, the Roman salt tax, are G. 18,000 ducats, B. 21,000, V. 14,000.

18. G. 12,000 ducats, B. 15,000, V. 15,000.

19. B. 10,500, V. 10,000.

20. G. 16,000, B. 10,000, V. no figure.

21. G. 8000, B. 12,000 (taken together with tax on grain), V. 13,000; these figures are uncertain since they are composed of different items in the various sources.

22. This tax comprises right of grazing in Rome *and* the Patrimony of St. Peter: G. 16,000 (seems very high and out of line), B. 9000, V. 8000. The Patrimony of St. Peter is the region north of Rome extending into Tuscany.

23. G. 10,000, B. 11,000, V. 9777.

24. For the deficits in the budgets of Alexander VI and Julius II, see Gottlob, *Camera apostolica*, pp. 263-265.

25. For a list of the chief collectors (Depositario Generale) from the early fifteenth century till 1513, when Filippo Strozzi took over, see Gottlob, *Camera apostolica*, pp. 111-112.

26. On the Spannocchi, see Ubaldo Morandi, "Gli Spannocchi: piccoli propiertari, terrieri, artigiani, piccoli, medi e grandi mercanti-

banchieri," in *Studi in memoria di Federigo Melis*, III (Rome, 1978), pp. 93-115; this article is based on a memoir about members of the Spannocchi family which can be found in Archivio di Stato, Siena (henceforth abbreviated ASS), section: *Archivi privati Spannocchi AI*. I have added some information that I found in other archival sources.

27. My facts about tax farmers in the time of Alexander VI and Julius II come chiefly from A.Vat., arm. XXXIV, vols. 11, 13, 15, 16.

28. For the situation in 1500, see the above-mentioned report dated October 28, 1499, ibid., vol. 11, f.1333r-336r.

29. On June 29, 1500, see the report published as the first appendix in Johannis Burchardi, *Diarium sive rerum urbanarum commentarii*, ed. L. Thuasne (Paris, 1885), III, 434.

30. Contract printed in *Cugnoni*, p. 209. The original is in Biblioteca Vaticana, *Archivio Chigi:* no. 3665 *(Pergamena)* (henceforth cited 'BV, Arch. Chigi).

31. Vittorio Franchini, "Note sull'attività finanziaria di Agostino Chigi nel Cinquecento," *Studi in honore di G. Luzzatto*, II (Milan, 1950), 157.

32. See A.Vat., arm. XXXIV, vol. 13, f.147v; vol. 15, f.21r-21v. Some further business contracts that Chigi concluded in 1495 can be found in BV, Arch. Chigi: arm. 290, no. 11453 (vol. VIII).

33. *Cugnoni*, pp. 14, 211.

34. A.Vat., arm. XXXIV, vol. 13, f.141r-142r, November 2, 1495.

35. *Cugnoni*, pp. 296-299.

36. *Cugnoni*, pp. 299-304.

37. Franchini, "Note," p. 156, note 2. The source is a letter of Agostino to his father, preserved in BV, Arch. Chigi: RVc., *Lettere diverse*.

38. See A.Vat., arm. XXXIV, vol. 16, f.25v, where on January 24, 1495, Franza appears as Chigi's procurator; Franza participated with Chigi in the farming of the Dogana Mercium and the Dogana di Ripa; see BV, Arch. Chigi: arm. 290, no. 11456 (vol. VI), f.352, f.364. Franza also assisted Chigi still in 1510 in a financial transaction securing the services of the Condottieri Vitelli for Venice; ibid., no. 3666 *(Pergamena)*, dated June 16, 1510.

39. On the payments to Alexander VI, see *Cugnoni*, pp. 109, 507. For Chigi's Tolfa contract see Delumeau, *L'Alun*, p. 97. For a close analysis of the contract, see O. Montenovesi, "Agostino Chigi, banchiere e appaltore dell'allume di Tolfa," *Archivio della R. Società Ro-*

mana, LX (1937), 111-112.

40. Morandi, "The Spannocchi," on pp. 113-114, mentions that, from the end of the fifteenth century on, the Spannocchi were interested in the sale of alum and even mining it. There is a document in ASS, *Giudice ordinarie,* V, no. 47, which shows that Chigi was acquiring alum rights near Massa in March 1501, and that this was done in collaboration with the Spannocchi and had the support of the "ruler" of Siena, Pandolfo Petrucci. This suggests that entering the business of alum mining was originally a common enterprise of the Sienese bankers.

41. The text of the contract is printed in Montenovesi, "Chigi," pp. 124-128; on Chigi's relations with his father, see Franchini, "Note," pp. 158, 161.

42. Burchardi, *Diarium,* III, 250, 252, and the contract of the cardinals with the Spannocchi is printed there, pp. 447-448; according to a later copy of the contract in ASS, *Archivi privati, Spannocchi AI,* 28, the firm of Stephanus de Chinucci participated in this loan to the cardinals. It ought to be mentioned that the Fuggers also helped the College of Cardinals to defray their expenses; see Schulte, *Fugger,* I, 33-34. Chigi also made a contribution of 1500 ducats against a security of gold and silver; see A.Vat., arm. XXXIV, vol. 16, f.64r, v.

43. Burchardi, *Diarium,* III, 245, 283.

44. See Pastor, *History of the Popes,* VI, 217-218.

45. See Montenovesi, "Chigi," p. 112.

46. For the rise of the Sauli, see Archivio di Stato, Roma (henceforth abbreviated ASR) *Fondo camerale,* busta 857, f.51r-61r (concerns dogana pecudum), f.77r-87v (concerns salt tax), or A.Vat., *Introitus et exitus,* vol. 548 (introit), f.18v, 62r. Paolo Sauli died in 1507, and Vincentius and Sebastian Sauli took over. Although the name of the Sauli occurs very frequently when you study financial affairs at the Curia under Julius II, my impression is that they controlled the financial apparatus of the Curia less completely than the Spannocchi had, and that there was more circulation among the tax farmers.

47. See Montenovesi, "Chigi," p. 112.

48. This was certainly the opinion of the contemporaries. See Guicciardini, *Storia d'Italia,* book VI, chap. 5, or the views of the Venetian ambassador Antonio Giustiniani, quoted in Brosch, *Papst Julius II,* p. 96; even Pastor, *History of the Popes,* VI, 209, writes that Julius "did not hesitate to have recourse to bribery."

49. On Chigi's management of the Tolfa mines, see Delumeau, *L'Alun*, pp. 103-106. See the material quoted in note 58.

50. The Spannocchi seem to have been the only Sienese firm with whom Chigi broke off contacts. Chigi maintained close relations with other Sienese businessmen—Ghinucci, Tommasi, Bellanti—and he was most anxious to serve the interests of Pandolfo Petrucci.

51. BV, Arch. Chigi: no. 3665 (*Pergamena*).

52. The Spannocchi's lawyer was the famous jurist Parisio, and his opinion on this case is printed in his *Consiliorum pars prima* (Venice, 1580). Chigi's argument was that the prolongation of the lease he had received from Julius II represented a new contract, so that the one concluded under Alexander VI was no longer valid; from 1505 on, Chigi had refused to give the Spannocchi a share of the profits. Parisio argued that the agreement made under Alexander VI had been concluded for twelve years and had remained therefore valid. The court followed Parisio, although the judgment was issued only after Chigi's death. In 1524, the Chigi were sentenced to pay the Spannocchi 200,000 ducats, according to Franchini's "Note," p. 170. Documents in ASS, *Archivi privati: Spannocchi AI* (*Pergamena*), show that the Spannocchi-Chigi litigation was not ended with the decision of 1524; negotiations continued into the 1540s, when some compromise finally seems to have been reached. The situation was complicated because not only did the Spannocchi have claims against the Chigi, but the Chigi also had claims against the Spannocchi.

53. In A.Vat. AI, *Introitus et exitus*, vol. 541, f.17, January 1507, the Ghinucci are mentioned as tax farmers on overland imports to Rome and in vol. 546, June 1509, as farmers of the salt tax of the Marches.

54. Schulte, *Fugger*, I, chap. 3, discusses the relationship of the sale of indulgences to the rise of the power of the Fugger in Rome.

55. BV, Arch. Chigi: no. 3666 (book 2; *Pergamena*), f.117, gives the decree by which, on December 31, 1510, the brothers Chigi are made treasurers of the Patrimony for five years; ASR, *Fondo camerale, prima parte: Libri decretarum camerae*, case 290 (1510-1511), mentions the Chigi as farmers of the tax on grazing, and of the salt taxes of the Marches and of the Patrimony (May, July, and December 1511). Sigismondo Chigi, according to BV, Arch. Chigi: arm. 290, no. 11456, f.335, together with two merchants from Siena, farmed the Gabella Studii (probably 1507).

56. The variety of Chigi's businesses emerges clearly from the documents and papers preserved in the Vatican's Chigi archives—for instance no. 3666 (book 2; *Pergamena*), f.53, for negotiations with Condottieri (1510), or arm. 290, no. 11451, for a cloth deal (1513), or nos. 341, 360, for contracts to set up with others a "compagnia d'arte di seta" (1508).

57. See ibid., no. 11453, f.368r-369r; this is well known. See Pastor, *History of the Popes*, VII, 189, and appendices 36-38, pp. 470-488, for the relevant documents.

58. The description of Chigi's methods in making the monopoly of the Tolfa alum mines effective is based on material contained in BV, Arch. Chigi: arm. 290, no. 11453, f.248 (agreement with Girolamo Buoninsegni on Sicily); ff.260r-263r (concerns Spain where Buoninsegni had some rights); f.272 (agreement with the Florentine Bartolini, giving them a monopoly for the sale of Tolfa alum in Provence and Aigues-Morte for three years).

59. The contract about Porto Ercole is printed in *Cugnoni*, pp. 422-434.

60. "Questo maladetto Porto Ercole . . .," letter of Chigi to Antonio da Venafro, March 13, 1513, BV, Arch. Chigi, RVc, *Lettere diverse*, f.15r.

61. From 1509 on, Porto Ercole becomes increasingly important as a port for the shipment of alum, and the "galione di M. Agostino Chigi" appears as vehicle on which alum is transported; see ASR, *Fondo camerale: Tolfa*, busta 2380.

62. For the difficulties in enforcing the papal alum monopoly in Christian Europe, see the second chapter of the first part of Delumeau, *L'Alun*; but the issue is also treated in Gottlob, *Camera apostolica*, pp. 278-305, and, with emphasis on the second half of the fifteenth century, in G. Zippel, "L'Allume di Tolfa e il suo commercio," *Archivio della R. Società Romana*, XXX (1907), 5-51, 389-462.

63. The agreement is printed in Montenovesi, "Chigi," pp. 135-140; the document is not dated but must be from 1506 or 1507.

64. The conflict between the government and the merchants of the Low Countries and Chigi is treated in detail by Jules Finot, "Le Commerce de l'Alun dans les Pays-Bas et le bulle encyclique du Pope Jules II en 1506," *Bulletin historique et philologique* (1902), pp. 418-431; some additional facts can be found in the succinct account by Delumeau,

L'Alun, pp. 36-38.

65. See these papal messages in A.Vat., *Julii II brevi,* arm. XXXIX, vol. 23; the dates of the brevi to the Doge Loredan are November 14, 1504, and February 20, 1505. They are filed in chronological order. The mission of Baptista Mauro is mentioned in the letter to the Doge of November 16, 1504, but there is another breve to Mauro, urging him to press the papal interests regarding the alum monopoly, dated September 30, 1505.

66. The material on which the description of the Pope's intervention in England is based comes from the chronologically organized volume 23 of Julius' *Brevi:* the relevant letters are to Henry VII, dated October 16, November 4, November 12 (contains the reference to the attitude of previous popes toward trade with pagans), 1505, March 29, May 15, 16, 20 (announces mission of Petrus Grifus); to the captain of the king's ship, Waring, September (s.d.), November 13, 1505, July 18, 1506; to the king's mother, May 16, 1506; to Grifo, May 15, 1506; to Polydore Virgil, May 12, 1506; to the Bishop of Winchester, May 16, July 12, August 6, 1506. See also *Letters and Papers Illustrative of the Reigns of Richard III and Henry VII,* ed. James Gairdner (London, 1881), II, 167-168. There were two incidents that stimulated papal action: the appearance of the king's ship *Sovaren* in the Mediterranean, sailing to Asia Minor in 1505, and the transportation of Turkish alum by the Florentines Frescobaldi and Gualterotti in 1506. The treatment in Gottlob, *Camera apostolica,* p. 302, is incomplete; the contract published in Montenovesi, "Chigi," p. 136, shows that Grifo's mission was followed by one of Tommasi. Delumeau, *L'Alun,* p. 46, and Montenovesi, "Chigi," p. 114, are very brief, mainly relying on Gottlob.

67. See the tables of alum exports in Delumeau, *L'Alun,* pp. 214-215.

68. The explanation of this encyclical is the chief point of Finot's article mentioned in note 64.

69. The correspondence with England leaves no doubt about this.

70. The documents on Chigi's acquisition of this chapel and the papal bull are published in *Cugnoni,* pp. 440-443.

71. The document can be found in BV, Arch. Chigi: no. 3666 (*Pergamena*), f.31. Morandi, "Gli Spannocchi," p. 103, states that Pius II granted the Spannocchi the privilege of adding to their name "dei Piccolomini"; it seems to me most likely that competition with the Spannocchi was an important motive in Chigi's actions.

72. See Christoph Luitpold Frommel, *Die Farnesina und Peruzzi's Architektonisches Fruehwerk* (Berlin, 1961), pp. 6-7, on the building of the Farnesina and on the inspection of the progress of the work by Julius II in July 1511. A description of the house in the Via de Banchi, in which Chigi had his offices and lived before he moved to the Farnesina, can be found in *Cugnoni*, pp. 488-490.

73. The demand is first reported in *Dispacci degli ambasciatori veneziani alla corte di Roma presso Giulio II*, ed. Roberto Cessi (Monumenti Storici pubblicati della R. Deputazione di Storia Patria Serie Prima: Documenti XVIII (Venice, 1932), pp. 36-37 (henceforth cited *Dispacci*); for the shock which the demands of the Pope caused in Venice, see *Sanudo*, VIII, cols. 510-511.

74. *Dispacci*, p. 89; also p. 123 for another discussion of Grimani with the Pope on the question of the "gulf."

75. Francesco Corner's report from Rome, dated October 30, 1509, is in *Biblioteca marciana*, VII, codice MCVIII (7448), ff.375v-379v; see also *Dispacci*, p. 145, and Brosch, *Papst Julius II*, p. 182, on Francesco Corner's audience; resume of reports from Rome in *Sanudo*, IX, cols. 298-299.

76. An excellent historical survey of the issues connected with the gulf is Antonio Battistella, "Il Dominio del golfo," *Nuovo archivio veneto*, n.s., XXXV (1918), 3-102; also Frederic C. Lane, *Venice* (Baltimore, 1973), p. 65.

77. For the Venetian remonstrations, see *Dispacci*, pp. 93, 150/1, 201. The reference to Biondo is to the eighth book of his *Decades secundae*.

78. *Dispacci*, p. 191. On the interest of Julius II in navigation and his attempts to build a papal fleet, see P. Alberto Guglielmotti, *Storia della marina pontificia*, III (Rome, 1886), pp. 67ff: the Pope exaggerated the size of the fleet he was building and played down the strength of the Venetian naval power.

79. See the text of this clause in the peace treaty between the Pope and Venice, published in *Sanudo*, IX, col. 583.

80. *Sanudo*, VIII, cols. 187-205.

81. It may be remarked here that, when the Venetians wondered why this demand was raised so late—as a kind of afterthought—the Pope referred only to some very general statements; see *Dispacci*, p. 70.

82. Ibid., p. 146.

83. Ibid., pp. 37, 150.

84. Reported in Guglielmotti, *Marina pontificia*, III, 57ff.

85. The dispute over whether Comacchio had come to the Este from the Emperor or from the Pope continued until the eighteenth century. Muratori wrote a treatise about this question in the interest of the Este: *Succinta esposizione delle ragioni del S.R. impero e della serenissima case d'Este sopra Comacchio* (1710).

86. *Dispacci*, pp. 197, 206, 227, mainly December 1509.

87. Pastor, *History of the Popes*, VI, 327ff, deals with Julius' conflict with Ferrara; it ought to be said that the Venetians continued the war against Ferrara and, in December 1509, burnt in Comacchio the installations for salt production; see *Sanudo*, IX, col. 395. See also Antonio Frizzi, *Memorie per la storia di Ferrara*, IV (Ferrara, 1796), 222.

88. Baronius (Raynaldus), *Annales ecclesistici*, XXX (Lusae, 1754), pp. 551-553.

89. The source is a letter from Leonardo da Porto, dated 1511, to Antonio Savorgnano, published in *Lettere di principi*, I, ed. Girolamo Ruscelli (Venice, 1562), 19v. Guicciardini, *Storia d'italia*, book IX, chap. 1, also underlines the importance of this issue in the Pope's conflict with Alfonso d'Este.

90. This statement is certainly exaggerated because Chigi had no monopoly of the salt tax in the entire papal state. However, he and his brother were farmers of the salt tax in the Patrimony and the Marches in 1511; see above, note 57.

91. Brosch, *Papst Julius II*, p. 255.

92. As a letter from Agostino to his brother, Sigismondo, written in Venice on May 18, 1511 (BV, Arch. Chigi, RVc, *Lettere diverse*, f.19v-20r.) indicated, the son of a friend of the Petrucci in Siena was involved, and Chigi was always very much concerned about remaining on good terms with the Petrucci.

93. There are four letters from Agostino to Sigismondo from Bologna, the first dated October 21, 1510, then from November 7, 11, 12, to be found in BV, Arch. Chigi, RVc, *Lettere diverse*, ff.16r-17r, 17r-18r, 18r-19r, 48r. Since there is a letter to Sigismondo, dated September 28, 1510, from Rome, Chigi must have gone to Bologna after the Pope, who had entered Bologna on September 22. There are no letters from Agostino between the letter to Sigismondo from November 12, 1510, and a letter from Venice on February 21, 1511. Undoubtedly there is the

possibility that, between Bologna and Venice, Agostino went for a short time to Rome, but considering the difficulties involved in traveling at that time, this is not likely and certainly does not change the argument. In addition to the letter to Sigismondo, dated February 21, 1511, from Venice, there are three other letters to Sigismondo from Venice, dated March 3 (ff.20r-20v), and two letters dated May 18 (ff.19v-20r, 20r). As far as I can see, the letters—very difficult to read—contain nothing about negotiations with the Venetian government regarding a loan and an alum sale; this might speak for the political aspects of the transaction because Sigismondo, in general, was kept informed of business affairs.

94. For the impact of the relations with France on the peace negotiations, see *Dispacci*, pp. 37, 41ff, 137ff.

95. The fact that, until the League of Cambrai, Maximilian had pursued a strongly anti-French policy, gave some likelihood to the possibility that Maximilian might abandon the French.

96. Although Venice changed from the anti-French to the pro-French side only two years later, in March 1513, there was some speculation about the possibility of such a move a long time before.

97. The most authoritative biography of Maximilian I—Hermann Wiesflecker, *Kaiser Maximilian I*—of which the third volume appeared in 1977, has not yet gone beyond the year 1508; Pastor, *History of the Popes*, VI (London, 1898), 344-348, gives the main facts about Lang's meeting with the Pope in Bologna and indicates the main sources. The most brilliant—and probably the best informed—discussion of these negotiations is found in Guicciardini, *Storia d'Italia*, book IX, chap. 16; Guicciardini indicates that the Venetian negotiators, under strong pressure from the Pope, finally agreed to cede most of the terra firma to Maximilian but to keep Padua and Treviso against payment of a great sum of money. But, to the great relief of the Venetians, the unwillingness of Lang to make any agreement about Maximilian's entering the war against France, led to a break and to Lang's departure from Bologna. The instructions the Venetian government sent to its "Oratori in Curia" are characteristic. Although they emphasize strongly the Venetian willingness to follow the wishes of the Pope, they also tell the Pope to distrust Lang and emphasize the bad consequences that an agreement with Maximilian might have for Italy as a whole; see ASV, *Senato secreta*, reg. 44, for instance, the instruction dated April 21, 1511.

98. See Augustin Theiner, *Codex diplomaticus dominii temporalis santae sedis* (Rome, 1862), III, ff.518-524. The conclusion of the alliance between Ferdinand of Aragon and the Doge of Venice—that is, the adherence of Spain and Venice to the Holy League—was witnessed by "spectabilibus viris dominis Augustino Chisio et Bartholomeo de Auria et Andrea Gentile mercatoribus Senensibus et Januensibus Romanam Curiam sequentibus testibus."

V. The Closing of the Account

1. The full text of Chigi's will can be found in *Cugnoni*, pp. 197-205; on p. 199 are the statements on the Villa Farnesina to which I refer in my text. Only one son of Agostino Chigi, Lorenzo, survived, and he had one son, Agostino, who died without issue so that with him the male line of Agostino ended. Lorenzo came into financial difficulties, and the family was forced to sell the Villa Farnesina. Agostino's brother Sigismondo had five sons, who moved from Rome back to Siena. One of Sigismondo's descendants was Fabio Chigi, who in 1655 was elected Pope and, in recognition of the favors the Borgia Pope Alexander VI had bestowed on his ancestors, took the name of Alexander VII. The Chigi family was now divided into Sienese and Roman branches. The Roman Chigis are "hereditary guardians of the Conclave"; they have played a prominent role in Roman political and social life.

2. For the analysis of the paintings in the loggia of the Villa Farnesina, see Fritz Saxl, *La Fede astrologica di Agostino Chigi. Interpretazione dei dipinti di Baldassare Peruzzi nella sala di Galatea della Farnesina* (Rome, 1934); as my interpretation shows, I place slightly less emphasis on Chigi's belief in fate than Saxl does. See also F. Saxl, *Lectures*, I (London, 1957), "The Villa Farnesina," pp. 189-199, and in general, Christoph Luitpold Frommel, *Die Farnesina und Peruzzi's Architektonisches Fruehwerk* (Berlin, 1961).

3. In general, see Eugenio Garin, *Medioevo e rinascimento* (Bari, 1954), particularly the chapter "Magia ed astrologia nella cultura del rinascimento."

4. Agostino's acquaintance with Pinturicchio's work is seen from a letter to his father, dated November 7, 1500: "Sopra la capella vostra . . . voi dite havere parlato con M⁰ Pietro Perugino, vi dico che volendo fare di sua mano Lui è il meglio maestro d'Italia e quale che li chiama il

Paterichio è stato suo discepolo il quale al presente non e qui: altri maestri non ci sono che vaglino" (BV, Arch. Chigi: RVc, *Lettere diverse*, I, f.14r-15r). Of course, the virtù-fortuna contest was a common issue of debate in the Renaissance; the Pinturicchio presentation of this problem is mentioned here only in order to establish a direct contact with Chigi, who, because of the decorations in the Villa Farnesina, is too easily characterized as a believer in astrology.

5. See Frommel, *Farnesina*, pp. 4-5, and the sources given in the footnotes.

6. On Chigi's artists, see Frommel, *Farnesina*, pp. 13-14.

7. The Aldus edition had been published two years earlier, but although the two editions overlap, each has material that is not printed in the other.

8. Aretino certainly enjoyed Chigi's grandiose hospitality; see Pietro Aretino, *Il Primo libro delle lettere*, letter 162 to Ferrieri Beltramo.

9. See the description in Fabio Chigi's life, in *Cugnoni*, pp. 34-36, and further details in Frommel, *Farnesina*, pp. 7-9. The various comments on Chigi in Sanudo's diary—after Chigi's departure from Venice (they are extensively used by Frommel, *Farnesina*, pp. 7 and 8)—seem to me more significant in showing the reputation that Chigi enjoyed than as actual facts.

10. For Chigi's loans to Leo X, see the documents published by Montenovesi, "Chigi," pp. 128-130, and Delumeau, *L'Alun*, p. 105. Although Pastor, *History of the Popes*, VII, 25, emphasizes that simony was not involved in Leo's election, it is likely that the 75,000 ducats borrowed for the coronation were connected to promises made at the time of the conclave. Chigi's financial support of Leo X continued throughout his reign; still in February 1520, two months before Chigi's death, we find among the Chigi papers—BV, Arch. Chigi: RVb, f.3—a notice that Leo X received 1500 ducats from Chigi and gave jewelry as security; another security Chigi received from his loan was a tiara. It ought to be remarked that the rise of the Medici to power in Rome placed not only a burden on Chigi; a notice, dated September 30, 1514, in BV, Arch. Chigi: arm. 290, no. 11453 (vol. VIII), f.309v, states that Alfonsina Medici, the widow of Piero, has repaid to Chigi the money he had lent earlier to the Medici, and that means particularly Piero.

11. The question why Chigi reduced his share in the exploitation of

the Tolfa mines, and allowed Andrea Bellanti to come forth as chief farmer, has been frequently discussed, with no good answers given. I make the following suggestions: (a) There was a legal reason: Leo X, on becoming Pope, declared that nobody was permitted to receive more than one lease from the Curia (Chigi was treasurer of the Patrimony); the purpose of Leo's decree, of course, was to make space for his Florentine friends. (b) The Bellanti were related to the Spannocchi; Cassandra, daughter of Antonio Spannocchi, was the wife of Antonio Bellanti; see ASS, *Archivi privati: Spannocchi AI (Pergamena)*, nr. 20. Some attempt to resolve the litigation with the Spannocchi might be involved. Such an assumption would be strengthened by the fact that, when Chigi resumed control over the Tolfa mines in 1520, the Spannocchi received a partnership. (c) I am convinced that Chigi was anxious to lead the life of a great noble, not that of a "mere" merchant.

12. See Delumeau, *L'Alun*, p. 98. Since Chigi died early in 1520, this change in the lease of the contract in 1520 clearly was a deathbed arrangement to secure control over the Tolfa alum for his heirs.

13. See *Cugnoni*, p. 204.

14. *Sanudo*, XXIV, col. 628.

15. "Bazarioto."

16. ASV, *Senato secreta*, reg. 43, October 22, 1519: "Oratori nostro in Urbe," "persona cautilata et cavillosa."

17. See the resume of Chigi's memorandum in ASV, *Libri commemoriali*, XIX, nr. 238.

18. For the discussions on this matter, see ASV, *Senato secreta*, reg. 44, December 14, 1511, and *Dieci misto*, reg. 34, f.169v, December 27, 1511; then *Senato secreta*, reg. 44, January 2, 1512, and Bibl. Correr, *Priuli*, VII, f.188v. Also, *Sanudo*, XIII, col. 369, which indicates that in the debate in the Pregadi on January 2, the contrasts of the summer came again to the fore.

19. ASV, *Libri commemoriali*, XIX, nos. 237, 238, 247; the printed resumes of the documents preserved in the *Libri commemoriali* are not always correct.

20. "E non li vien observati li soi capitoli," *Sanudo*, XXIV, col. 422, July 1, 1517. From the year 1514, we have—in ASV, *Capi del consiglio dei dieci, lettere di ambasciatori* (Rome, 1513-14), busta 21—a letter from Pietro Lando, the Venetian ambassador in Rome, dated Septem-

ber 4, in which it is said that Chigi urged him to find out from the Venetian government "come el si die governar," after he had received no answer to a first request. This may refer to complaints about the appearance of other alum on the Venetian market, but this is speculative; it is possible that Chigi had suggested negotiations about the agreement in general. The archives contain no further material from this time on the matter.

21. I have used the Italian translation of Andrea Mocenigo's "War of the League of Cambrai," printed in Venice in 1543, where the passages I discuss are on pp. 139r-140r.

22. The law that had allowed the auctioning of offices was abolished immediately after the end of the war.

23. See Lester J. Libby, Jr., "Venetian History and Political Thought after 1509," *Studies in the Renaissance*, XX (1973), 7-45. I have treated this issue also in my "Venice in the Crisis of the League of Cambrai," *Renaissance Venice* (London, 1973) pp. 289-290, and in my "Religion and Politics in the Thought of Gasparo Contarini," in *History: Choice and Commitment*, pp. 247-267.

24. *Sanudo*, XXVII, col. 210.

25. See ASV, *Libri commemoriali*, XX, no. 105.

26. ASV, *Capi del consiglio dei dieci*, busta 22, and *Sanudo*, XXVII, col. 409.

27. See ASV, *Libri commemoriali*, XX, no. 106, and letter from Alvise Gradenigo to Domenico Trevisan, September 10, 1520, in ASV, *Capi*, busta 22.

28. ASV, *Libri commemoriali*, XX, nos. 109, 110.

29. See Chigi's ratification document in ibid., no. 113, but see also his draft of this document in BV, Arch. Chigi: arm. 290, no. 11453 (vol. VIII).

30. See ASV, *Senato secreta*, reg. 48, August 23, f.45r, and *Sanudo*, XXVII, col. 582.

31. See ASV, *Senato secreta*, reg. 48, August 28, for draft of an instruction that was not sent.

32. Ibid., September 29; also *Sanudo*, XXVII, col. 668, for a discussion on this instruction. See also for the change in Cardinal Corner's power of attorney, ASV, *Libri commemoriali*, XX, no. 115.

33. See also *Sanudo*, XXVIII, cols. 20, 35, and ASV, *Senato secreta*,

reg. 48, instruction to Cardinal Corner, dated October 22, 1519; also ASV, *Libri commemoriali*, XX, nos. 119, 120.

34. For this and the following, see ASV, *Senato secreta*, reg. 48, instructions to Cardinal Corner and the Venetian ambassador in Rome of November 29 and December 22, 1519; also *Sanudo*, XXVIII, col. 37.

35. *Sanudo*, XXVIII, cols. 111, 128-129, and ASV, *Senato secreta*, reg. 48, letter to Cardinal Corner, December 22, 1519.

36. ASV, *Senato secreta*, reg. 48, instruction to the Venetian ambassador between December 22 and December 28. The files contain this instruction in two forms; the one proposed by the Council of Savi, the other by two Savi of the terra firma; for the differences and the discussion on the instruction, see *Sanudo*, XXVIII, col. 129.

37. For this and the following, see *Sanudo*, XXVIII, col. 129, and the instructions to the Venetian ambassador mentioned in the preceding note. They are followed by a third letter to the Venetian ambassador, probably from the same day, which explains in detail that Chigi had made a gain of 30-32,000 ducats as a result of his agreement with Venice. They arrived at this figure in the following way: Chigi sold in Venice within eight years 4000 cantari of alum at a price of 20 ducats for one cantaro; at other places, he sold alum for 11 and 12 ducats a cantaro; consequently, he earned on each cantaro sold in Venice 8 ducats more than he made in other places like Ferrara; this then amounts to a surplus earning of 30-32,000 ducats.

38. See ASV, *Capi*, busta 22, report of Marco Minio, dated January 26; since Cardinal Corner's letters are lacking, the material is very incomplete.

39. See ASV, *Senato secreta*, reg. 48, instruction to Minio, dated February 16, 1520, and *Sanudo*, XXVIII, col. 260, 265.

40. *Sanudo*, XXVIII, col. 320.

41. Ibid., col. 340. The Pope found compliance with Chigi's demand difficult for legal reasons.

42. Michiel's letter is published in *Sanudo*, XXVIII, col. 424-426; Michiel, of course, is the so-called Anonimo Morelliano.

43. For a description of his funeral, see *Sanudo*, XXVIII, col. 424; a more detailed description is given by Frommel, *Farnesina*, p. 12.

44. ASV, *Libri commemoriali*, XX, nos. 131, 133-136, 138, 140, 142. In *Capi*, busta 22, there are a number of letters from the Venetian am-

bassador in Rome, Alvise Gradenigo, to Domenico Trevisan "equiti et procuratori di San Marco" in September 1520, mostly in cipher but evidently concerned with the return of the single pieces of jewelry.

VI. Julius II: Caesar and Vicar of Christ

1. I use the translation by Leonard F. Dean in the University of Classics edition, first published in 1946. In the Leyden edition of Erasmus' *Opera omnia*, this passage can be found in IV (1703), 484. For contemporary impressions of Julius II, see also Loren Partridge and Randolph Starn, *A Renaissance Likeness: Art and Culture in Raphael's Julius II* (Berkeley, 1980).

2. For Erasmus in Italy, see Augustin Renaudet, *Erasme et l'Italie* (Geneva, 1954).

3. From Erasmus' letter to Cardinal Domenico Grimani, May 15, 1515; the quoted passage can be found in the *Collected Works of Erasmus*, III, 94, *Correspondence*, letter 334, trans. R. A. Mynors and D. F. S. Thomson (Toronto, 1976).

4. Erasmus to John Botzheim, 1523, in *Opus epistolarum Des. Erasmi Roterodami*, I, ed. P. S. Allen (Oxonii, 1906), 37. See also Carl Stange, *Erasmus und Julius II—Eine Legende* (Berlin, 1937), pp. 28-29; this book contains valuable material, but its interpretation of the development of Erasmus' views regarding war and Julius II cannot be accepted.

5. Erasmus' authorship of the *Julius Exclusus* can no longer be doubted. For a recent discussion of Erasmus' authorship, quoting the relevant literature, see *Collected Works of Erasmus*, IV, 169, *Correspondence*, introduction to letter 502. See also James K. McConica, "Erasmus and the *Julius Exclusus*, a Humanist Reflects on the Church," *The Pursuit of Holiness in Late Medieval and Renaissance Religion*, ed. Charles Trinkaus with Heiko Oberman (Leiden, 1974), pp. 444-483.

6. Erasmus to Leo X, May 21, 1515, *Collected Works*, III, 102-103, *Correspondence*, letter 335.

7. For the origin and the sources of this woodcut, see David Rosand and Michelangelo Murraro, *Titian and the Venetian Woodcut* (Washington, D.C., 1976), pp. 37-5ᵈ lso Erwin Panofsky, *Problems in Titian Mostly Iconographic* (New Y , 1969), pp. 58-63. Titian's woodcut is assumed to have been done in 1510 or 1511. Allusion to the Holy

League is possible only if the woodcut was done in the later part of 1511, but allusion to a war conducted jointly by the Pope and Venice is possible throughout 1510 and 1511.

8. I use the translation of the *Julius Exclusus* by Paul Pascal (Bloomington, 1968), where the remark can be found on p. 49.

9. In the translation by Leonard F. Dean (see note 1), p. 112; in the Leyden edition of Erasmus' *Opera omnia*, IV, 483-484.

10. Bibl. Correr, *Priuli*, VI, f.313r.

11. For a recent discussion of the expectation of a Golden Age at the time of Leo X, see John W. O'Malley, "The Discovery of America and Reform Thought at the Papal Court in the Early Cinquescento," *First Images of America*, ed. Fredi Chiappelli (Berkeley, 1976), I, 185-200, and also his "Fulfillment of the Christian Golden Age under Pope Julius II: Text of a Discourse of Giles of Veterbo, 1507," *Traditio*, XXV (1969), 265-338.

12. See Jean Delumeau, *L'Alun de Rome, XV-XIX siècle* (Paris, 1962), part 3.

13. With the exception of Cremona, which was kept by Milan, and two small places along the Isonzo, which Maximilian received.

14. On the Venetians' tendency to transform their past into a myth, see my "Venetian Diplomacy Before Pavia: From Reality to Myth," in *History: Choice and Commitment*, pp. 295-321.

Index

Adriatic Sea, 18, 26, 53, 54, 85, 86, 87, 90. *See also* Gulf
Agnadello, battle of (1509), 1, 2, 16, 44, 45, 56
Aldus Manutius, 102, 111
Alexander III (Orlando Bandinelli), pope (1159-1181), 86
Alexander VI (Roderigo Borgia), pope (1492-1503), 15, 54, 69, 71-75
Alexander VII (Fabio Chigi), pope (1655-1667), 64
Alfonso d'Este, duke of Ferrara, 88, 89, 90
Alidosi, Francesco Cardinal, governor of Bologna (1511), 52
Alum, alum monopoly. *See* Tolfa
Alviano, Bartolommeo d', condottiere, 27
Ancona, 53, 66, 86, 88. *See also* Gulf
Aragon. *See* Ferdinand
Aretino, Pietro, 98
Arimondo, Alvise, 24
Arimondo, Marco, 58

Baglioni, 66
Balance of power, 115, 116
Balbi, Pietro, 43, 46, 62
Bankers, banking houses, 34, 65, 67, 75, 97, 103, 116. *See also* Cappello-Vendramin; Chigi; Fugger; Ghinucci; Pisani; Priuli; Sauli; Spannocchi; Tommasi

Bellanti, Andrea, 98
Bellini, 57
Bembo, Bernardo, 17, 25, 62
Bembo, Pietro, 74, 88
Bentivogli, 52, 66, 68
Bergamo, 27
Besalù, Raphael, 15, 57, 62, 77, 105
Bibbiena, Piero Dovizzi da, 74
Biondo, Flavio, 87
Bologna, 3, 52, 54, 55, 66, 68, 91, 92, 111, 112. *See also* Alidosi; Bentivogli
Boninsegni, Girolamo, 78
Borgia, family, 69, 73, 74, 75. *See also* Alexander VI; Calixtus III; Cesare
Bramante, 98
Brescia, 27
Bruges, 80, 83
Burckhardt, Jacob, 65, 66

Calixtus III (Alonso Borgia), pope (1455-1458), 69
Cambrai, League of, 1, 4, 6-9, 12, 18, 26, 36, 81, 85, 102, 111-117
Campagna, province in papal states, 66
Cappello, Venetian patrician family, 62. *See also* Cappello-Vendramin
Cappello, Lorenzo, 17, 26
Cappello, Paolo, 31, 32, 34, 44
Cappello, Piero, 17, 26
Cappello-Vendramin, Venetian

153

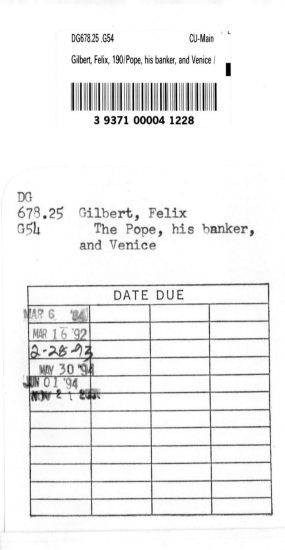

DG
678.25   Gilbert, Felix
G54   The Pope, his banker,
         and Venice

DATE DUE			
MAR 6 '84			
MAR 16 '92			
2-28-93			
MAY 30 '94			
JUN 01 '94			
NOV 2 (2001			